The Burglary Business and You

PETER BURDEN

The Burglary Business and You

M
DIPLOMA

To all burglary victims

Line illustrations by Chris Evans

© Peter Burden 1980

ISBN cased edition: 0 333 30499 3
ISBN paper edition: 0 333 30500 0

First published 1980 by
MACMILLAN LONDON LTD
London and Basingstoke
Associated companies in Delhi, Dublin,
Hong Kong, Johannesburg, Lagos, Melbourne,
New York, Singapore and Tokyo

Published in association with Diploma

Phototypeset in Great Britain by
Filmtype Services Limited, Scarborough
Printed by Billing and Sons Limited,
Guildford, London and Worcester

Contents

Introduction

Did you know that the burglar is at work in Britain, on average, once every minute of every day and night of every week? Some of the hardest-working burglars have police records which list hundreds of offences. Convictions are not deterrents, for those who are caught receive light sentences. Burglars simply go on growing richer and richer by stealing other people's property, making the burglary business Britain's biggest single criminal industry.

There are several good reasons why burglars are so enthusiastic about their work. Apart from the fact that a burglar does not expect to end up behind bars unless he is persistently caught, the truth of the matter is that official government statistics show that very few burglars get caught in the first place. On a national basis, only a third are arrested each year, in some areas far less. In London the rate is only just over one in ten.

Burglary has become a massive industry – an organisation comparable with the huge nationalised industries, with healthy export records apart from a good home trade. In this industry businessmen who appear to be totally respectable place the orders for goods to be stolen – from paintings and antiques to wine and chocolate; receivers act as the middle-men, placing the orders with suitable burglars; and the whole cycle often ends with unsuspecting members of the public purchasing the stolen goods – sometimes in High Street shops.

Commerce has reacted to all this by spending millions of pounds on security to deter burglars. The burglar in turn now concentrates more and more on the less well protected – the house and flat.

While no one can stop the burglary business from continuing to boom, more and more private citizens, despairing of the inadequacies of hard-worked, overstretched police resources, are taking their own actions to beat the burglar. Many are successful, but those who do deter the burglar from entering their own home simply send him elsewhere.

1

Once upon a time the penalty for burglary was death by hanging on the public gallows. In more recent times – from 1916 – burglary carried the deterrent of swingeing prison-sentences – up to a maximum of life imprisonment. No burglar appearing before a judge at an Assize or Quarter Session could expect to leave the dock to face a future of anything but a long stay in jail.

But from 1962 – the time when serious crime in Britain began its leap to today's high levels – punishment for burglary was effectively lessened. One Act of Parliament after another was passed, each in reality reducing both the length of the prison-sentence for burglary and the risk of imprisonment as punishment at all. Finally, the Criminal Law Act of 1977, which came into effect in 1979, takes the country into the 1980s allowing burglaries to be dealt with by local magistrates – and not even necessarily by the higher courts at all.

Britain's most outspoken and most respected policeman, Sir Robert Mark, former Scotland Yard Commissioner, was the first to spell out the realities behind the mounting statistics reflecting the booming burglary industry. He spoke out as the deterrent of punishment for burglary declined and the volume of burglaries escalated to such a degree that its sheer numbers swamped the police machinery. Sir Robert deliberately chose a meeting of security experts attending a seminar organised by AGB Conference Services to declare that the police could no longer properly protect the public against thieves. For too long, he said, the public had lived in a world of growing pretence, and the time had come for them to assume the responsibility of protecting their own property. His speech on 17 October 1978 lifted briefly, and for the first time, the veil that covers the modern social phenomenon of the burglary business. The shock waves of his words were felt far and wide – and no less significantly in senior police circles.

Now, although much of the dust has settled, it is worth recalling the key points of Sir Robert's speech in 1978.

> Anyone reading the reports of the Chief Inspector of Constabulary and the Metropolitan Police Commissioner may reasonably draw at least two general conclusions. The first is that so far as crimes against property are concerned – that is, burglary, breaking offences, theft and dishonest handling – the police in England and Wales have probably reached their lowest point in effectiveness in living memory. The second is that this situation is more than twice as bad in London as in the provinces. Only 6600 or 9.8% of 67,500 aggravated burglaries and burglaries from dwellings were cleared up in London last year (1977), the corresponding figure for the provinces being 67,300 or 34% of 195,000. . . .

As police ability to prevent crime diminishes, the inducement to insure against loss from it increases. . . .

The simple truth is that crimes against property are now so numerous that both police and courts are of little relevance from the point of view of the victim and the insurer. . . .

I am suggesting quite bluntly that for the first time in this century the belief that the State can, or even wishes to, protect people effectively from burglary, breaking offences and theft should be abandoned, at least in the great cities, where inadequate numbers of police have other and much more demanding priorities.

Strong words indeed from Britain's most influential policeman. Furious Yard chiefs made reassuring noises to the public. They had not abdicated their responsibilities. They had not abandoned the householder to the burglar. Counter, but unconvincing, statistics were made available to the media. Scotland Yard officers made no secret of their feelings. Sir Robert, they hinted, would be more helpful to their fight for law and order in difficult times if he would kindly keep quiet.

The truth of the matter, then, was that the police were doing their very best against burglars. There were, and are today, burglar squads at work in the hardest-hit areas. These teams of 'commando'-style detectives assigned to make impact do just that. The arrest rate in these areas is high. Their successes cannot be ignored. But these squads, when viewed in a national context, are making only a pinprick of an impression. When the home of a prime minister is burgled or there is an outbreak in an area in which VIPs reside, the police react very positively. But these small squads of specialists put into the hardest-hit areas are only carrying out 'fire-brigade policing'.

A fact of life is that burglary flourishes because police have inadequate resources – and this crime is not high on their list of priorities. The main resources of the police are now limited to containing crimes of violence. Police chiefs say that the gunman on the street, the mugger and the rapist are the criminals who cause the most public disquiet. Burglary has become accepted as an unwelcome but integral part of urban society.

Since Sir Robert spoke out, there has been a convenient levelling-out in serious crime nationwide. Even burglary has shown a decrease over all. At least, it appeared to have dropped in 1978, but a closer examination of the statistics reveals that, as far as the householder is concerned, this is not the case. Household burglaries have increased, but the over-all figure shows a drop because of positive action taken in the commercial sector. Many millions of pounds are spent by commerce every year to protect the factory, the office and the shopping-precincts from the burglar. The security guards, the sophisticated alarms, the specially designed doors and windows – indeed, the very design of premises – all help to deter the burglar, but these moves have not put him out of business.

When police set up special anti-burglar squads in one residential area, the thieves soon move operations to another less-protected vicinity. So, too, with commerce. As commerce has responded to the unacceptable, so burglars have turned their attention more and more to domestic premises – the house and the flat. Today, a burglary is being committed every minute of every hour of every day. In reality, the rate is higher, because the one burglary every minute is a calculation based on the ones that are known. Committed on this scale, it is natural that burglary should have generated an entire industry of its own.

Insurance payouts are a not insignificant clue to the annual turnover. Insurance payments in respect of burglary rose from £9 million in 1973 to £37.9 million in 1978 – and that relates only to household policies. In 1978 there was an additional £18.3 million compensation paid out by the members of the British Insurance Association for theft-losses at commercial and industrial premises. Taking into account the estimate that 25% of households are not insured, and that these figures relate only to companies which are members of the BIA, then at an intelligent guess the real turnover in the burglary business annually can be put around the £100 million mark – all untaxed profit.

In the following chapters we take the first-ever in-depth look at the whole spectrum of the burglary business. The victim – from the rich to the pensioner whose carefully saved-up coins to pay for the electricity bill are not immune from the grabbing hands of the burglars; the world of the burglars – ranging from the specialist antique gangs who rob to meet a worldwide demand to the schoolboy who breaks into his classroom to steal the geography books he hates; the huge commercial industry – which has developed to make it possible for the millions of pounds of stolen goods to be so easily recycled; the insurance world – which has alleviated the individual loss on the one hand with compensation and, by so doing, has encouraged public acceptance of the crime; and, of course, the hunters – the police and security men, who are trying like King Canute to stem the tide, and with about as much effect.

In the case of victims, actual surnames and locations of homes have been omitted. Information about security of individual premises and valuables kept at home could aid burglars who would read these contents with as much interest as the law-abiding general public, the police, security organisations, and insurers. All possible steps have been taken to ensure that this publication is not a burglar's guide to crime.

At the same time, the true identities of burglars whose activities are set out in depth cannot be given because of the possibility that they will be facing fresh criminal trials for crimes committed since the writing of this book. Full revelation could lead to claims prejudicial to a hearing – particularly before a jury in the event of a Not Guilty plea.

Nevertheless, although exact names are not used, every account relates to actual incidents and persons involved in the business of burglary.

PETER BURDEN

1 The Victims

Barbara

The moment Barbara turned the key and opened the front door of her £100,000 home in north London at four o'clock on a November afternoon she knew her worst fears had been realised – she had been burgled.

Nothing in particular had singled out that day to be the most traumatic in her life. Her sister was here on a visit from France, and they had left at 2.00 p.m. to visit a physiotherapist. Her husband, Bernard, the chairman of Europe's largest market-research company, was at his desk in the City of London, having been driven to his office by his chauffeur, George, after breakfast. The sisters had left together with Barbara's son, Paul, aged twenty-four, a young lawyer. He was representing a client at the local magistrates court. The other son, John, aged twenty-two, had been indulging in his culinary hobby and was baking bread before leaving for a planned round of golf followed by a social visit to Wasps, his Rugby club. The daily had been at work. It was her final task, if the house was empty when she left at about 2.00 p.m., to set the burglar-alarm switches, thus securing the premises.

The house, standing amid three-quarters of an acre of well-kept gardens, with a swimming-pool, was in a quiet avenue. It was the home of a successful family. That fact that it was a likely target for burglars had not been overlooked. There were two burglar-alarm systems – one covering the front half of the house, the other the rear. The alarm-bells in their boxes had been prominently positioned by experts, high on the outside walls. They were not linked to the local police stations but designed to activate alarm-bells that could be heard by neighbours in the event of a break-in at a window or door. The family's policy and hope was that the noise of the alarm-bells would be a great deterrent to any would-be burglar. For good measure, a third brightly coloured alarm-box had been positioned by the chimney. It appeared to be genuine, but it was empty – just a dummy to act as an additional deterrent. The burglar precautions had increased with the family – the first system was installed when they moved in twenty years ago, the second and the dummy as the family prospered and grew richer over the succeeding years.

When the daily had left the house at 1.45 p.m. she had not switched on the burglar-alarms, for she believed that the son, John, was still indoors baking bread. She had not actually seen him, but she had looked into the kitchen and seen that all his bread-making equipment was out on the stove as though about to be used. As far as she was concerned, he was definitely in the house when she left.

A team of professional burglars were 'working' the neighbourhood as she walked down the drive. They called purely by chance fifteen minutes later. They pressed the door-bell and, if anyone at home answered, they would use one of their many cover-stories as an excuse – 'Have you any antiques for sale?' or 'Have you considered double-glazing?' Then they would leave promptly and try elsewhere.

Receiving no reply, the raid was on. A stepladder left lying on the ground outside the laundry was used to reach the burglar-alarms. Wirecutters severed the leads to the alarm trigger-points at the windows and doors. The alarms were wrenched from the walls. The team knew they were not of the type with a back-up link via the telephone system to the local police station. They did not know that the alarm system was switched off.

The second the alarms had been neutralised, a downstairs ground-floor bedroom-window was forced open. The burglars were men of long experience – total professionals. They knew that once inside the house every second counted. Grab everything worth while as you move from room to room in case you are disturbed and have to depart in a hurry with what you have.

It took only minutes to ransack the first bedroom. Every drawer, with its neatly stacked contents, was yanked out and hurled on the floor, as were the contents of the wardrobe. Being professionals, the burglars brought no sacks to remove the haul – a chance meeting with the police on the way would have resulted in embarrassing questions and hurried and unconvincing explanations, which would have added unnecessary risk. Why take sacks when there are pillowcases on beds? And most homes have a ready supply of suitcases stored in attics for family holidays. The gang stuffed the pillowcases with every item of value they could find. A golf-grip in the wardrobe was emptied of shoes and then used as an additional carrier.

Mink coats, jewellery, money, credit cards had top priority. No other clothing apart from the mink was touched – too bulky. As the team moved around the house they found the cocktail-cabinet well stocked. They did not pause to touch a drop, but removed a leather case of brandy tots. That had resale value. A Black & Decker torch and power-handle were taken: the gang could obtain a far better price for those than for a few bottles of liquor.

Unlike amateurs, or hooligans on a break-in, there was no wilful damage or vandalism. That wasted time. Within minutes, a member of the team had found the rows of family suitcases stacked in a storeroom. The raiders were in the lounge now. The silver was stuffed into the cases. They ignored the more bulky pictures on the wall. Picture-stealing is a specialist crime. There was, however, no hesitation about the videotape recorder worth £750, or the portable television in the breakfast-room. There is an instant market for such items. The Victorian wall-clock – almost irreplaceable – was removed from its brackets.

It turned out to be a worthwhile haul. Nothing too spectacular – about £8000 to £10,000 worth of highly resaleable goods. In fact, the haul was better than expected; the problem was to get all the goods into their Range Rover, which had been parked a short distance away, just around the corner at the end of the road. While one member of the gang went to fetch the vehicle, another found an unexpected bonus. In a cupboard close to the garage he spotted a set of car-keys with the unmistakable Ferrari tag. In the garage was a £15,000 twelve-cylinder six-carb Ferrari.

Stealing a Ferrari is not the business of a burglary gang – it is too easily identifiable, and trying a quick sale of a stolen quality car courts disaster – but the gang was heavily laden with goods and, being opportunists, they realised that the car did have its use – even if only for half an hour. The overspill from the Range Rover was bundled into the Ferrari. The driver was ordered not to speed and they drove to a rendezvous-point in Bayswater. There the goods were transferred and the 'hot' car abandoned. It had served its purpose.

The gang had swept through the house in less than half an hour without drama. A little sweat as they raced against the clock, but no incidents. When the lady of the house opened her front door at four o'clock, the real nightmare began. She immediately dialled 999. A young plain-clothes policeman arrived ten minutes later as Barbara was alerting her husband in the City. Bernard ordered George, his driver, to be at the entrance of his office-block immediately for a fast drive home. As Bernard drove home, the first officer at the house was joined by a detective sergeant. Their expert eyes took in a scene which, on diverse scales, occurs in the Metropolitan Police area at least once every few minutes of every day, day in, day out.

Barbara was still trying to assess exactly what had been taken when Bernard arrived home at 5.15 p.m. She stood among piles of

9

family possessions tossed from drawers. The full shock of the rape of her home had not yet settled in. Her husband noticed the garage doors were open as he drove in. That was when the police first knew that a £15,000 Ferrari had been stolen. It now became more than just a routine burglary.

The man of the house may have been chairman of a huge business organisation, but he was not a VIP politician or a showbiz star. The burglary would not make the national press – the volume of such crimes had long since devalued their importance – and the police knew that crime reporters at the Yard would have said 'Thanks, but no thanks' if given the item as news. Possibly the local paper could appeal for help from local residents if nothing else showed up from police checks in the vicinity. It was certainly not a case for a priority telex over the police internal system for the Yard HQ.

The Scenes of Crimes Officer had arrived by 5.15 p.m. to give the two detectives back-up. 'SOCOs', as they are affectionately known, are civilians brought in as much-needed help to the overstretched resources of the force officers. It did not take the SOCO very long to report that it was 'an all-glove job'. The only scientific evidence was a scuff on the ground-floor bedroom-wall by the window which confirmed that as the point of entry.

Barbara began the harrowing job of preparing an inventory of items stolen. The detectives began to build up a picture of the family routine that day. The cheerful SOCO helped ease the tension with some anecdotes and general principles of how burglars worked.

Then – suddenly – the telephone rang. The caller asked Bernard, 'Are you satisfied with your burglar-alarm system?' Was it a sadistic call from the burglars? Incredibly, it was from the service department of the burglar-alarm firm saying it would be some days before they could be around to check over the equipment on the annual service. It was a routine call – the man was totally unaware that there had just been a burglary. The caller gave his name and number, and a quick return call from the police confirmed it was all an extraordinary coincidence.

By now the two detectives had pieced together an outline of the family and were seeking explanations in order to eliminate the obvious. They had noticed an old VW parked in the drive. To whom did it belong? Bernard explained it belonged to his elder son, Paul. Bernard somehow knew what the policemen were thinking. In a house of top-quality cars, a young son owned only an old VW. Could he have carried out the burglary to get his own back on the family for some reason? Was he a dropout? He was not at home. Bernard's explanation that theirs was a united happy family temporarily satisfied the officers. However, Paul could only be totally exonerated after he returned home.

10

What about the home help? The fact that such a question had to be asked about the long-trusted family friend and servant confirmed the hovering suspicions. Both officers were diligent, and as polite and helpful as they could be. But the questions had to be asked – and answered. The 'daily' was located. Then came the bombshell: she had not turned on the burglar-alarms, because she was sure that John had been at home when she left.

There was no trace of him. True enough about the bread-baking equipment. It was, as she said, on the stove. It appeared to have been abandoned in the middle of cooking. Barbara's sister put what everyone was thinking into words: 'I don't want to start anything, but aren't you worried? He said that after baking he would go to golf and be back at 4.30.' The time now was nearly six o'clock. As Bernard later told me: 'We were all sick with worry. Had my son been at home when the raiders arrived? Had he returned early from golf? Was he a kidnap victim?'

The detectives circulated an all-cars alert for the vanished Ferrari. Now they were urgently seeking the full details of the BMW John was driving. A routine burglary was taking on much more sinister overtones. Maybe the Yard should be alerted after all. But the detectives had first to be sure there was not a simpler explanation. George, the driver, was sent to the local golf club and then on to the Rugby club. There was no sign of John. The burglary now looked very secondary.

Suddenly it was over. John's car swept up the drive. He had been in the golf club tea-room. That had been overlooked in the hasty check. Paul, who had taken tea with a client after a court case, arrived fifteen minutes later.

'From the moment John arrived home safely, I took the conscious view that I didn't care a damn about the burglary – it could have been all that much worse. It was such a relief,' said Bernard.

His immediate reaction was relief that his son was unharmed. It is, of course, a key reason why burglary does not have the highest priority-rating for the police. And burglars know that they are doubly benefited by not getting involved in any type of violence during a raid. Any violence automatically 'ups the ante' at the courts: the sentence is increased, and the chances of ending up in court are higher because a burglary with violence attracts much more police priority attention. So the burglars who raided Bernard's home had no thoughts of violence towards the family, and were unaware of the later, but brief, anxiety John's absence caused.

The real loss for that family was entering the second stage. They were back to wondering who had done it, and what had become of their possessions – among them many treasured personal items. Bernard said, 'A burglar throws suspicion on everyone. You end up suspecting yourself. You begin to feel under suspicion. Was the burglary an insurance fiddle? You know that must have crossed the police minds when they asked about the cover you have got.'

For Barbara the burglary entered another phase. She knew exactly what had been taken. She itemised a growing list:

	£		£
1 mink jacket	900.00	silver shoe-horn (antique)	20.00
14 ct gold locket	164.50	silver candlestick	15.00
9 ct bangle bracelet	140.00	2 silver coasters (magnum	
silver oval locket	25.00	size) @ £100	200.00
gold brooch locket	42.50	1 silver round hand-mirror	35.00
silver hinge bangle	30.00	silver filigree brooch	20.00
9 ct oval gold locket with		1 silver coaster	
chain	160.00	(medium-size)	25.00
silver rope link 28"	22.00	1 gold crucifix	15.00
silver swizzle-stick	27.00	1 gold-leaf necklace and	
silver cocktail-stick,		chain	25.00
engraved	23.50	1 pearl link necklace with	
silver necklace	26.50	diamante ring	30.00
silver leaf-design brooch	6.50	1 matching 2"-wide bracelet	10.00
18 ct gold Victorian ring		mother-of-pearl gilt brooch	10.00
(rubies and diamond)	85.00	orange/brown costume	
gold dress ring with smoky		brooch	5.00
quartz	40.00	black 3-link necklace	10.00
18 ct bracelet, Milanese		yellow and gilt chunky	
mesh	40.00	necklace	8.00
9 ct slave bangle (round		earrings – about 12 pairs @ £2	24.00
hollow)	50.00	1 mink collar (black)	50.00
5 ct slave bangle (fancy		1 single pearl necklace	
pattern)	50.00	(choker)	25.00
charm bracelet	69.50	1 single pearl necklace	
identity bracelet, silver	20.00	(long)	30.00
pearl necklace and earrings	15.00	1 antique silver	
silver sugar-castor and jug		powder-compact	50.00
(antique, Wateling)	150.00	1 Glama mink (1973	
Georgian silver cream-jug	20.00	valuation)	1,175.00
4 silver napkin-rings @ £9	36.00	1 leather grip	40.00
2 matching silver ashtrays		1 large green leather case	50.00
@ £20	40.00	1 Black & Decker	
2 silver leaf-design dishes		power-torch	30.00
(matching) @ £25	50.00	1 Black & Decker	
1 silver rose-vase	25.00	power-handle	10.00
Wedgwood oval brooch	34.00	2 plated ashtrays @ £15	30.00
stainless-steel watch	28.50	1 plated cigarette-box	25.00
amber necklace set	76.50	leather jewel-box	25.00
agate bracelet	31.00	Thwaites & Reed	
dress ring with turquoise	24.00	bracket-clock	600.00
blue agate signet-seal ring	28.50	man's full-length suede coat	350.00
1 silver christening-mug	35.00	brass carriage-clock (Roman	
small silver jug (1890)	25.00	figures)	50.00
silver button-hook 12"		brass carriage-clock	
(antique)	20.00	(English figures)	50.00

	£		£
brass perpetual clock	45.00	1 pewter tankard	20.00
3 brass ashtrays	10.00	1 plated coaster	15.00
Chinese brass bowl		1 walnut sample kneehole	
(antique)	25.00	desk (antique)	200.00
Chinese brass dish (antique)	25.00	2 bottles scotch	8.00
brass dish on stand	15.00	1 single bedspread	
Spode flower-seller (c.1940)	100.00	(cashmere)	25.00
binoculars in leather case	80.00	2 pillowcases @ £2	4.00
opera glasses in leather case	35.00	1 plated coffee-pot (ebony	
man's gilt watch	25.00	handle)	20.00
exercise-wheel	10.00	1 oval pot with silver lid	25.00
Sèvres snuff-box	25.00	1 broad gilt bracelet	15.00
£70 in £10 notes	70.00	gilt choker necklace	25.00
£30 in foreign currency	30.00	gilt twisted necklet	14.00
crystal fob-brooch	50.00	diamante bracelet	10.00
2 × 12″ matching Sheffield		6 pewter brandy-tots in	
candlesticks (antique)	120.00	leather case	20.00
1 plated bonbon-dish	15.00	1 plated coaster	6.00
glass dish with silver		steel bracelet	5.00
embossed lid	10.00	burglar-alarm damage	30.00
1 round plated ashtray	15.00		
1 plated engraved jug			
(Lebanese)	30.00		

By the weekend Barbara wanted actions, results. Items with precious family meaning were gone. Bernard made constant phone calls to the police for news, but by Saturday his burglary had dropped to fifth place on the detectives' workload chart. A rape superseded it. 'I already knew at that stage that neither I nor the police had an earthly chance of identifying the burglars and getting our things back,' recalls Bernard, 'but Barbara wanted to do something. She felt so helpless.'

Soon they were on the heartbreaking trail taken by so many thousands of burglary victims – the tour of the street-markets and auction-rooms. Their eyes were those not of buyers but of hopeful spotters of personal possessions. 'I thought going to the Portobello Road market on the Sunday was a terribly forlorn chance, but I decided to go along with anything that would alleviate Barbara's frustration,' said Bernard. 'The problem was now really in the mind. It was hurting. And she felt it was really helping not to be passive. You just have to go out and help yourself. But it's like doing the Pools. You want the jackpot, but the odds against you are so enormous. You ask yourself where the burglars could sell your goods. You know they are around somewhere. The hours spent stalking through the markets and antique-shops did help. It gave the wounds time to heal, at least a little.'

The insurance men came round. Many items had been under-insured. The minks had not been up-valued to keep pace with inflation. The insurance people paid out at the old prices, and the family settled down to rebuild. But the theorising and guessing went on. The friendly milkman – could he have given the burglars the tip-off? What about the firm of building contractors working down the road? What about the door-to-door salesman who had been in the area? The suspicions might well have remained for ever, as they do in the majority of cases, except for a lucky break. All the items in the list prepared by Barbara had been collated at Scotland Yard's central index of stolen property. Two weeks later, two silver napkin-rings were recovered from the boot of a car in a totally unrelated enquiry. They were enough to convince the police that Bernard and his wife had been the victims of a team of professional burglars whose method of operation was simply to knock at the doors of suitable premises and, if no one was at home, to burglarise them. That at least removed the clouds of suspicion that had fallen on people in the neighbourhood.

Shelley

Nine-year-old Shelley came face to face with her burglar when a slight noise in the darkened bedroom disturbed her sleep. She opened her eyes and looked straight up into the face of a strange man. Neither said a word. She vividly remembers that the stranger paused, turned on his heels, and walked quietly out. Above all, she recalls he was wearing white plimsoles and blue jeans. She is unable to describe the face or other features. Shelley cuddled up tight against her 'snugglie', a favourite woollen doll, slid down deeper into the warmth of her bed, and went back to sleep.

Her encounter with the burglar cost her a sharp ticking-off when in the morning she ran into her parents' room with her exciting story. 'Mummy, Mummy, there was a man in my room last night.'

Her mother, Hannelore, a hospital sister in her late thirties, told me: 'I said I did not believe her. I said she had been dreaming. I wasn't pleased at all because it was Saturday morning, my day off, and I had been up late the previous night. It was not until the milkman knocked at the door about half an hour later that I discovered Shelley had been telling the truth and that we had been burgled. The milkman needed paying and I went for my handbag which I had left in my bedroom by the side of the bed. It just wasn't there.' Also missing was the bicycle of her elder daughter, Camilla, aged twelve. It had been parked in the hallway.

Close examination revealed no obvious sign of forced entry, other than scratches by the front-door lock. The conclusion was that the burglar had picked the front-door lock and let himself in. The haul was £37 cash, and a cycle worth about £34. The handbag was found in bushes close by. So was the family-allowance book. 'We started getting jittery – it was the second time we had been burgled since moving into town from the country,' said Hannelore.

For the first twelve years of their eighteen-year marriage, she and her husband, Tony, lived in Wokingham in Surrey. 'We never worried about burglary then,' said Tony. 'Once we even went on our annual holiday and left the french windows open by mistake. Nothing happened. We joked about what the burglars had missed when we returned from holiday, but in those days it was only a joke. We did not have to worry in those days. But it is a different story now.'

The family moved in 1975 to a house in a small inner-London development of fifteen properties. The houses are close together – with land at a premium in the area the builder had utilised every square foot. This factor alone initially gave the families in the development a sense of security.

For the first three years there were no incidents. Then, in 1976, came the first burglary. There had been a dinner-party for friends on Saturday night. At 1.00 a.m. they retired, deciding to leave all the dishes and glasses until the morning. The guests stayed overnight.

'We had cut glasses in those days,' recalled Hannelore. 'I remember we lined them all up along the window-ledge in the kitchen. We were tired. We had just ended a good meal with plenty of wine and we did not want breakages. So we said we would leave everything. Because of the cooking-smells I left the kitchen-window slightly open.'

While they slept, a burglar opened the window wide and carefully removed the wine-glasses from the window-ledge, placing them on the ground outside. He then climbed in. Hannelore had left her handbag in the lounge. There was £30 in her purse. The guests had more cash – £60 – in a handbag left just inside the bedroom door.

'The first we knew we had been burgled was when a neighbour knocked in the morning and suggested we pick up our cut glasses, which were lined up on a communal footway running past our kitchen-window.'

Until that first burglary they had taken no precautions at all. In fact they had not even considered they were exposing themselves to risk by leaving a ground-floor kitchen-window open. 'After that we started making sure we locked doors and shut windows,' said Tony.

A year later came 'Shelley's burglar' – an event which left the family jittery.

Nine months later, while the family were out for the day, there was another unwelcome visitor. Again, entry was believed to have

15

been by the front door. A purse and a wallet and the family's 'petty cash collection' were taken. This time the haul was £100. There was no damage. But this time the insurers fussed. 'They simply wrote to say they no longer wanted to reinsure us,' said Tony. 'To be fair, it was not just these burglaries. We had also had a small loss claim. So our record read three burglaries and a loss claim. They no longer wanted to know. We got reinsured very easily – and the joke was that the new premium was smaller than the one we had been paying before. We pay a premium of £113 a year – that's a replacement for new contents, and we are covered for any personal losses outside the house as well. For example, if my wife lost her coat while out at a restaurant, we would be covered.'

The new policy had not been in force long when there was a claim. Thieves forced open the boot of Tony's Cortina parked outside and removed the spare wheel, plus Camilla's fold-up bike.

A few months later burglars returned, and this time the raid was more serious. The visit was in broad daylight – between 11.00 a.m. and 2.00 p.m. while the house was empty. The intruders scaled a rear fence and, using a slab of wood, smashed a ground-floor rear window. The haul was a music centre, electric razor, woollen rug, alcohol and a hold-all – presumably used to carry the goods away. The total value was £391.

The raiders had struck while the new au pair girl was out shopping. They had had an unexpected windfall. The postman had been by since the au pair had left the house, and the burglars opened the five letters. In one, addressed to the au pair girl, was £25 in notes sent by her mother.

The burglars tried, but failed, to force the colour television from its large stand. Television and stand were too large to take out through the broken window. The burglars had tried to force the front door open; but after the last burglary an extra lock had been fitted, and even from the inside it could only be opened with a key. So there was no easy exit.

Now the family have locks on every window. Tony is installing a 'do-it-yourself' burglar-alarm which he bought for £80. The smashed window has been replaced with glass containing wire mesh.

'What Sir Robert Mark said was so true,' said Tony. 'There is little or no public protection. Do you know that when we called the police on the last burglary they said at the local station we were the thirty-third that day. They were very helpful, but after the initial visit there was no more interest. What could the police do? The only answer is to look after yourself. We are now resigned to the situation.'

Said Hannelore: 'Burglary has made an impact on our very way of life. When we lived in the country we never had to worry. I suppose

16

it may not be the same there now. But here I find I have lost peace of mind. If I am at home, and the doorbell rings, I now worry: Is it a burglar testing to see if anyone is at home? And no way will I let the girls return to an empty home. I could not stand them finding we had been burgled – or, worse still, coming face to face with a robber. I make sure I am always here now.'

I asked Tony how many of his neighbours have been burgled. His immediate reaction: 'Let's work out who hasn't.' He tots up. Over half, he reckons. Then he tells the favourite story which highlights the price the community is paying. 'Look at that house over there. See the iron bars on the windows and the metal spikes on the wall? Do you know that because of the burglaries here that owner has made his home into such a fortress that he says his big worry now is that he may not be able to get out if there is a fire at night?'

Muriel

Muriel's home was a pleasant three-bedroom detached house in a suburb of Manchester. The family, consisting of two girls and a boy, had been raised there. One had already left home, and the day was not far off when the other two would leave for London and the start of their careers.

The house now lacked for nothing. The expensive days of schooling and providing for a growing family were over. The husband's salary as an engineer provided holidays in Spain, a year-old family-car, a colour television (not rented now, thanks to a bargain offer in a January sale), and the lounge even boasted a corner with a 'bar' complete with two stools.

Life was good until Muriel, returning from a shopping expedition in the city centre, found she had been burgled. It was bad enough that the french windows in the rear dining-room had been forced open and £20 cash in the kitchen-drawer stolen; but the damage and vandalism aged Muriel on the spot, inflicting a mental wound even time would not heal.

A booted foot had shattered the television screen, leaving smashed glass, dangling wires and a jumble of crushed miniature valves. The three-piece suite had been up-ended and the fabric slashed – possibly in the hope that money had been hidden inside. Houseplants had been torn from their pots and hurled against walls. There was a horror in the kitchen. Three fish were dead on the floor, their heads stamped and crushed; they were from the family's small aquarium. The actual fish-tank was not broken – it was constructed of tough plastic – but it had been knocked from its stand and the water had soaked the fitted carpet. Kitchen-drawers had been yanked out and the contents strewn over the floor.

It was the same story in each room: devastation. But there was worse in Muriel's own bedroom. A lipstick had been used to scrawl obscenities across the walls and across the large mirror on a dressing-table. It took a little longer for Muriel to take in what had happened to her bed. It had been used as a toilet – smeared excreta and a large wet patch full of the stench of stale urine. Muriel retched on the spot and was physically sick seconds later in the bathroom. Her mental anguish was possibly no less horrific than if she herself had been raped. Muriel and her daughters spent that night away from the house. They stayed with horrified neighbours.

The next day began the task of cleaning up. Surprisingly, much of the damage was quickly repaired: the spilt water from the aquarium dried; paint obliterated the lipstick messages on the walls; insurance money provided for a new lounge suite. But what could not be eradicated from her mind was the picture as she walked through the house. It was a re-creation of those minutes when she discovered she had been burgled and vandalised.

She found she could not sleep. The extra sherry at night did not work. The doctor later prescribed tranquillisers. Ultimately her husband made the only decision he could. They had to sell and move from the home where they had planned to spend the rest of their lives.

The tragedy is that each year there are many thousands of Muriels.

At the Office

The sight that greeted Claire as she opened the door of her office in Newcastle on a bright spring morning stopped her dead in her tracks. She was the personal secretary to the marketing director of a car-sales organisation. She prided herself on her neatness and efficiency; but as she stood in the doorway with a freshly purchased bunch of daffodils in her hand she saw her world turned upside down – literally. Her polished wooden desk, which she had fought to retain when the company had moved into a modern office-complex and the plastic-coated furniture that went with it, was upside down on the carpet tiles. Her typing-chair was upright, and nothing else was out of place. But the thin wood of the base of the drawers in her desk had been smashed open – the heel of a booted foot stamped downwards had been sufficient to splinter the plywood into fragments. The remnants of the contents of the drawers – pencils, paper-clips and notebooks – were scattered nearby on the floor, and gone was the old tobacco-tin that contained the £3.70 tea and coffee fund.

But Claire's trauma of discovery that her office had been visited by burglars was little to that experienced by her boss. The electric typewriter and the dictaphone had also been taken. By the time replacements had been delivered and the police had departed after taking formal statements, a whole day's productivity had been lost.

This case is typical of the office burglaries that have become so numerous that the most publicity they can rate is hopefully a brief mention in the local newspaper. In reality they are a major source of unrecognised commercial disruption.

For example, in Glasgow a burglar forced open a rear window of the office of a firm of estate agents. The only item of value he found in a desk-drawer was a partially used cheque-book belonging to the company. When the burglary was discovered, the estate agent had to contact his bank, inform the manager of the cheques already issued, and explain that the rest had been stolen. He was asked by his bank to reissue on a fresh cheque-book all the cheques already in circulation. The bank explained that they were sending out warning and 'stop' notices to all banks in the area for cheques bearing the serial numbers of the entire stolen book.

In Guildford in Surrey burglars raided the offices of a local council depot. They stole petty cash – and then discovered in a store-cupboard twenty-two pairs of rubber boots and fourteen pairs of shoes available to workers employed out of doors. The value was a mere £500, but the inconvenience and disruption in work-schedules was much more.

In a Manchester office burglary the culprit could find nothing of value – until he noticed the office vending machine. His haul was less than £20, but it meant that no member of staff could enjoy drinks 'on tap' for several days.

Fire-escapes and washroom-windows are among the favourite points of entry to offices, but a surprising number of offices are burgled simply by the raider 'leaning heavily' on an insecure door. It is surprising what burglars take from offices in Britain's major cities. During 1979 items included radio 'bleepers' for executives, calculators, two-way radios, mobile generators for emergency use in case of power-cuts, and even electric clocks and fans.

2 The Burglars

The Story of Darren

Darren is just twenty-two years old, and already Scotland Yard has a bulky dossier on him at the Metropolitan Police Headquarters, Westminster, only ten miles from his home. He has seventeen convictions, the first chalked up when he was only eleven years old. He is a typical case of a schoolboy who was drafted into the booming business of burglary and either could not or would not get out. This is the story of his life between the ages of eleven and twenty-two, a period which deals in depth with the making of a professional burglar. It is just one story from the many thousands of similar cases which today pack the police files.

Darren is, to use the police classification for race, 'Identity code one', which means he is a white boy. He is just over six feet tall, strong, well built, fair-haired and clean-cut. For all but the last few years he has lived with his parents on the sixth floor of a high-rise block of flats on a council estate in Putney, south-west London. When he was in his late teens they despaired of him and refused to accommodate him any longer. Since then he has lived with a variety of girlfriends, when he was not behind bars.

Burglary has become a way of life for Darren. So far it has not paid off substantially, although he has graduated from robbing electricity-meters to specialising in burglary of antique-filled homes – a subject which, incidentally, he learned a great deal about during a period in Borstal.

His first conviction was at the local juvenile court in 1968. He had 'jumped' school lessons and was using the time in an attempt to rob the electricity-meter of a neighbouring flat when the housewife, who had been out shopping, returned home and caught him red-handed. He explained to the police he was really doing it for a 'dare' because 'all the other lads are at it'. As it was his first offence, and considering that he was only eleven years old, the woman magistrate looked sternly at Darren, gave him a motherly lecture, and told him she was letting him off lightly with a conditional discharge of twelve months. Darren was told that this meant that if he kept out of trouble for the next twelve months the incident would be forgotten as far as the law was concerned, but that if he appeared before the court again during that time he faced double trouble.

The hopes of the juvenile court, his parents, his teacher, were soon to be dashed. Darren had taken the first step on the path of burglary.

Meanwhile, the police had opened a criminal record file on him. His detailed description, address, details of parents, home and school had been systematically entered. Details were held centrally at the Yard and at the local stations in Darren's area. The home beat officers – the police constables responsible for patrolling his district (a mixture of concrete jungles of high-rise council estates and highly expensive detached homes of the rich) – were all made aware of Darren's existence.

One officer had just read Darren's details before setting off from the station on patrol when he spotted the boy. Darren was not breaking in this time. In fact it was not Darren who initially caught the PC's eye at all. It was the two other boys with whom Darren was walking in a local shopping-arcade. Both of Darren's associates – each a year older than he – were already well known to the PC as boy burglars. Each had been caught three times. Each had a file similar to the newly opened one on Darren.

The PC turned his attention to Darren, remembered the new file, walked on, and at the end of his patrol on his return to base he logged the intelligence that he had seen the three boys together. A separate entry went on each boy's file. The object was that, if any of the trio were caught crime-breaking, the police would have up-to-date knowledge of associates – and each would immediately come under suspicion.

The year 1970 was only a few days old when Darren, short of cash after the Christmas and New Year festivities, tried again. The unlocked door of a council flat near a friend's home provided the opportunity to slip inside. Rent money of £3 in the teapot, a record, and a bottle of gin – total value £11 – was the haul. But he was spotted by a neighbour as he left. All the police had to do was pick him up, and a few days later he was back at the local juvenile court. The magistrate was told of his conditional discharge – the twelve months had fortunately expired – and Darren was given a stern lecture and put on probation for two years.

So, at the tender age of twelve, Darren already had two convictions. The second conviction was added to the intelligence file at the local stations. 'A bad lad in the making' was the assessment of the local detectives. It was only a matter of weeks before Darren received his first 'pull' – police slang for stopping and questioning. It occurred on a street near Tooting late on Saturday night. The officer acted because Darren was 'known', but Darren had not been breaking the law. The 'pull' by the police was noted and a new entry made on Darren's intelligence file. 'Satisfactory explanation, when stopped,' the officer reported.

It was not the machinery of police and intelligence files which next brought Darren before a court. Only a few weeks after Darren had become a teenager the caretaker of the local boys' club spotted him leaving with two of the club's toolkits. Police said later that if he had taken only one, then it might not have been reported to them. But two was a distinct theft. Darren's explanation was that he had intended to take them and sell them at a local 'swap shop' to raise cash.

So Darren was once again back before the juvenile court. This time the magistrates decided that action was needed. They sentenced him to a total of twelve hours at an attendance centre. This meant Darren had to report to a centre, where he was given 'social' jobs, such as cleaning windows on several days in his spare time, until he had performed duties for a total of twelve hours.

Darren was now really on the road to crime. He was well and truly caught up in the machinery of law and order. He was, in fact, on probation for the £11 burglary – and he had broken his probation. Next day, after receiving the twelve-hour attendance-centre punishment, he was back before the magistrate for the breach of probation to be dealt with. He was given a conditional discharge and a further twelve hours at an attendance centre.

At the local police stations, these events were recorded – and the whole force of local officers now knew Darren. For he had proved to be 'active'.

We must give Darren his due. He did try hard during the summer months to keep out of trouble. He was becoming aware of his manhood and turning his attention to girls. But, as all schoolboys find to their cost, girlfriends are expensive. Even those girls who pay their way need to be impressed. What better way (Darren's thoughts would run) to impress a new love than with a motorcycle?

By October 1970, Darren was infatuated as only thirteen-year-old-boys who have grown up too soon can be. Marie needed to be impressed, and a brand-new Honda motorcycle was Darren's answer. For days he was the envy of his mates as he roared around on the new bike. But every yard he rode he was at risk. The bike had been reported stolen and was on the logs of area traffic cars. Late in October he was spotted as he rode with his Marie on the pillion seat.

When the police patrol-crew loudspeaker ordered him to stop he did, and both he and his girlfriend, to use the police phrase, 'decamped'. The trouble with Darren, of course, was that he was now too well known to get away with this sort of trick. The police knew him. They found him at home. The girl was allowed to leave after she, in tears, pleaded she had no idea that the Honda had been stolen. So our burglar-in-the-making now faced different types of charge: unlawful taking of a motor vehicle, driving without insurance, and driving whilst disqualified by reason of age. It was nearly Christmas and, as Darren found, magistrates are human. They decided to give him another chance and awarded him a conditional discharge – backed by a severe warning about the dangerous path he was taking.

As Christmas approached, Darren again faced fresh expenses for his favoured life-style. So it was back to burglary on the way home from school. An unlocked door of a terraced house, tried at random, presented no problems. Darren was soon furiously applying a screwdriver to the gas-meter. His haul was twelve shillings, but the price he was to pay when the police found his fingerprints was much higher. He was back at the magistrates court within three days. There he found the goodwill had finally run out. He was committed to an approved school for three years. First, he went to an allocation centre and, again, the workers whose job it was to rehabilitate the boys tried hard. They put Darren on his trust and allowed him home for Christmas.

Darren did have a good Christmas. His parents (his father was a bus driver and his mother a school cook) both had time off work. They had time to make the holiday festivities a family occasion. His parents did all they could to help their son. He enjoyed the leave. Mother gave Darren a fond farewell at the end of it. He waved goodbye clutching a food parcel. And he checked back into the approved school in good time.

As the days dragged by, Darren made a decision. Approved-school life was not for him. Two months after Christmas he absconded. His break-out was in reality simply a carefully timed walk-out. His freedom was brief. Without really thinking the escape business through, Darren simply headed for home. The approved-school headmaster notified the police. When a constable called at Darren's home a few hours later, the boy was recaptured without any trouble.

The approved-school staff must be given due praise. On his return they went out of their way to try to help the thirteen-year-old boy in their care. The housemaster had a long talk with Darren and approved his returning home legitimately by giving him weekend passes. That worked well for four weekends. On the fifth, Darren decided not to return. He also learned his lesson about the dangers of home while an absconder. At the end of the fifth weekend, he told his parents he was returning to school. Instead, he went to stay with 'friends' (i.e., his pals who were making out nicely in the field of burglary). Darren's freedom lasted six weeks. The teenage gang of four worked well. The eldest, aged sixteen, was the driver. That no one had a licence was of no consequence, for every car they used was stolen.

Darren was in action with his team, forcing a window at the rear of a terraced house in Earlsfield, only a few miles from his home, when an alert neighbour spotted them. She phoned the police. Responding to the 999 call, the squad car caught Darren and friends red-handed. At the police station, Darren confessed that he was an absconder. He also volunteered, when questioning began about his movements during the last six weeks, that he had lived by burglary. He revealed twelve incidents in which he had taken part, all similar crimes: breaking in to a flat or house by forcing a window or door with a screwdriver, then a hunt for cash, drink, radios, portable televisions – anything easy to carry that could be resold with no problem. Darren pointed out that because of his age the resale prices obtained for the goods from 'friends' was rock bottom.

He had spent his fourteenth birthday on the run. When he appeared at the juvenile court the day after his capture it was his seventh appearance. This time he faced one main charge of burglary – the offence at which he had been caught red-handed. The second charge was allowing himself to be in a motor vehicle knowing it was stolen. In addition, he asked for twelve cases of burglary 'to be taken into consideration'. The court was told by the police that but for his confession to the twelve burglaries they would still have been on the police files as 'unsolved'.

It was obvious to the magistrates that Darren could not be returned to the approved school which he had left. Instead, he was sent to a detention centre for three months. The more military-style discipline of the detention centre might teach Darren a short, sharp lesson, the magistrates hoped.

The detention centre, from which there was no easy escape, certainly appeared to work. Darren, in fact, was an ideal prisoner. He responded to the disciplined, orderly life. He mixed well with other boys and kept out of trouble. After two months of excellent behaviour, he was judged fit for an early release.

As Darren walked through the detention-centre doors, the staff were sending out a report of his release to the police (routine in all cases). The move is designed to help people like Darren. The police, who will have known of his sentence and that he was an escaper, might otherwise detain him again as a suspect escaper. But the information is an added item to his personal file at the local station.

The bigger and thicker the dossier, the more interest the police take.

Within two weeks a keen PC, just promoted to plain-clothes duties as a temporary detective constable, spotted Darren as he walked the streets of Wandsworth late at night. The officer stopped and questioned Darren and his friends. They all gave satisfactory explanations. They had been to a rock club and were returning home. The information was the latest entry in Darren's swelling police file.

For the next few months all went well. Darren attended school, occasionally. His truancy from school did not help. Police cannot force children to remain in school, but schoolboys walking the streets during school hours obviously attract police interest. By November 1971 Darren's police file contained numerous entries: 'Stopped in Wandsworth High Street – should have been attending school.'

Another encounter between Darren and the police occurred in December. A PC stopped a car which was not displaying a road-fund licence. Darren was a passenger. The car was first thought stolen because there was no notification of the change of ownership. But it had not been stolen. The driver was prosecuted for not having a road-fund licence, and the incident became the latest report on Darren's police file.

In January 1972, three months before Darren's fifteenth birthday, his involvement with the police took a fresh twist. He became involved in a gang fight. Knives were used. Initially, Darren, along with the other youths, was charged with attempted murder, because a rival was seriously cut. Later the charge was dropped, and Darren was convicted of possessing an offensive weapon. He was bound over on his own recognisance of £25 for twelve months. It was a near thing, but it was not Darren's fault. He had become caught up in a brawl.

The brawl had been 'across the water' in north London. While waiting nearly a year to have the case heard, he was subjected to police restrictions when he was given bail after being charged. He was forbidden to cross the Thames from the south into the north-side territory. The police warned him that if he crossed the river he would be arrested for breach of bail. That was not too inconvenient. What annoyed Darren most was the second condition. It was that he should report daily to the police at 7.00 p.m. while on bail. On Saturdays, however, the police insisted that he should report at 4.00 p.m. Darren was a keen Crystal Palace Football Club supporter. All his mates attended the Palace matches. The police had insisted on the 4.00 p.m. reporting-time on Saturdays in a bid to keep Darren (then facing a serious knife-charge) out of the company of other youths whom the police saw as very undesirable. They did not want

Darren to contribute to a more serious incident on the soccer terraces on a Saturday.

Darren's fifteenth birthday came and went. It was not a good year for him. He was now very well known to the police. He was being regularly spotted by patrolling officers, and his movements and associates continually logged. If Darren did commit any more crimes during 1972, the police did not find out. The nearest he came to appearing before the courts was towards the end of the year when he got into a fight. Police were called to a brawl outside a pub. Darren was arrested at 2.00 a.m., but the complainant eventually declined to press charges and Darren walked free.

The new year of 1973 was barely a few days old when Darren was again in trouble with the law. His parents were by now despairing of their son. He was stopped while driving a car. Of course he was under age, did not have any insurance, and initially refused to give the police either his name or his address. He was fined £30 and disqualified until February 1974. Darren had no trouble paying. He had offically left school the previous summer and had a job working as a meat packer in a local factory. That job provided fifteen-year-old Darren with a good life. Not just the pay, of course. It was the sideline business which he had joined which made the real money.

Darren knew the licensees of two pubs. Each pub had a really lucrative lunchtime trade. The attraction for the customers was the meals. 'The best steaks in town' was the boast. The meat was certainly good, and cheap. The landlords, of course, could afford to keep the prices low, for they were buying meat that Darren and friends were stealing while at work.

This little business venture did not last long. His sixteenth birthday was celebrated back at the juvenile court, the charge 'handling stolen goods'. As it was his birthday, the magistrates released Darren on bail and adjourned the case for a fuller hearing at a date to be fixed.

Back to work for Darren. His next job was delivery boy. This job at least got him out and about. It was also excellent cover for his other activities. These 'other activities' were burglaries. This, Darren had decided at the experienced age of sixteen, was where the real money was to be found.

Within two months he had come unstuck again. An early-morning 'car-stop operation' by police netted Darren. This time he had a colour television which he had just stolen in a house burglary. This arrest put Darren in a new category. He was still aged sixteen and the top age at which youths can appear at juvenile courts is seventeen. However, this time Darren had been arrested with a friend who was eighteen – an adult. Because of this, the police took

26

the case to a magistrates court. It was the first time Darren had appeared in an adult court. He had come of age.

There was no escape with just a fine this time. After his record of previous convictions had been revealed the punishment was a sentence of six months at a detention centre.

The day after he had been booked into a detention centre, the prison van came to collect him for a day out. It was a trip back to court. The car incident had to be dealt with. He had been the driver on the burglary trip, but he had been disqualified until 1974. In addition, he had been driving a car without the owner's consent – he had simply 'borrowed' a friend's vehicle without asking. Of course he had no insurance. He was fined £5 with the option of one day in jail concurrent with each of the three charges. He paid up immediately and returned to the detention centre.

The matter of handling stolen goods remained in the pipeline. He was released early in 1974 from the detention centre, and a court fitted in his outstanding case. The sentence this time was Borstal.

Darren had graduated from approved school to detention centre, and now he was a Borstal boy. Ironically, it was in Borstal that he learned a trade that was to help him become a specialist burglar. He joined a class in Borstal that trained boys to learn a trade skill. The course was in restoring furniture. Darren became an enthusiastic pupil. He told his instructors of his keenness for antiques. He even obtained books from the Borstal library on antique furniture. He explained that he wanted to try to become an antique restorer.

The knowledge he gained in Borstal was to be put to full use. In the years to come, he was to commit burglary using his Borstal-acquired knowledge of which antiques to steal and which to leave behind. But, first, Darren had the problem of Borstal itself. Apart from his interest in learning all about antiques, he did not like being 'inside' at all. Christmas was coming and he wanted out. Two weeks before Christmas Day he escaped and was put on the police Wanted list. He remained free until February 1974, concentrating on making money from burglary. Between December 1973 and February 1974, when he was rearrested, he had taken part in an incredible ninety-eight burglaries. He was arrested when disturbed on the ninety-ninth.

The system was simple. He and a colleague first found a suitable car. Once stolen, false number-plates would be screwed on and the genuine ones ditched. They would then drive out of London – the bigger houses in Surrey and Oxfordshire were the attractions now, for many contained antiques. Darren had learned that antique dealers were queuing up for goods and asked few, if any, questions other than the price and date and time of delivery.

Darren by now, of course, was becoming an expert, more of a professional. He was becoming much harder to catch. The fact that he carried out ninety-eight successful burglaries before getting caught is significant when compared with his record as a young teenager. When Darren started on the burglary trail, he was arrested on his first break-in. As he grew up, so he became more artful in his crimes.

This is supported by Scotland Yard arrest-figures. In 1978, the clear-up rate for burglary was 10%, but nearly half of the 13,000 arrested were aged between ten and sixteen years. As the burglars mature, so the arrest-numbers decrease.

Darren evaded capture during his crime spree by taking precautions. For example, one stolen vehicle for a 'job' was no longer sufficient. Darren realised that every hour he used a car increased the chances of its being reported missing and detected by the police. So the refinement was *one* stolen car *to* the scene, locate and steal a second vehicle for the *return*, then carry out the crime. The more respectable the car, the better: a nearly-new family car, such as a Volvo, attracted far less police attention than a battered old car without a road-fund disc.

Normally, Darren was very careful when at work. He was all too well aware that the police had his fingerprints on record and that, after each burglary, a check was usually made by police for prints left behind. Usually Darren wore gloves.

His downfall this time was beer. He had stolen a van to drive to Surrey for the ninety-ninth burglary, and after such a good run of crime he had plenty of ready cash to spend. There were a couple of stops on the way to the target area; the early evening was passed away over convivial pints with his team-mate.

Hours after the pubs had shut, the suitable house was located. No lights or obvious burglar precautions. No barking dog. In fact the burglary went exceedingly well. He wore gloves as usual. But those pints of beer presented him with a human problem. Maybe they had mellowed him as well, for when he went to the toilet he took his gloves off and lifted the toilet-seat cover.

When the burglary was discovered, the housewife knew immediately that her toilet had been used. The flush had not been pulled. And a clear set of right-hand prints was on the seat.

Darren had by this time returned home to the London suburbs, unaware that the police were listing him as not only on the run but also wanted for burglary. Home was, in fact, the flat of a friend. The friend was not living there – he was in prison for theft – but he had left behind an attractive young wife. Darren had cash, not only for beer, but also for good living. He could support a girl in some comfort. He and Liz had gone to bed shortly after he first crossed the

28

threshold of the council flat in the high-rise block and he had discovered the fate of the husband. Liz may have conceived first time; she was certainly three months pregnant when she broke the news to Darren. Her biggest worry was how to explain her predicament to her husband when he came out of jail next year – and she could see difficulties about visiting coming up in the months ahead.

Maybe this had spurred Darren on to work so hard at burglary. He was to become a father. Darren accepted the position until he was arrested; he had been spotted by an off-duty constable in plain clothes who happened to have arrested him before. So it was back to Borstal. The problem of the baby was left by Darren to Liz. He had his own more urgent problems.

He had already learned there was no point in only being convicted for the one burglary for which he had been arrested. If the past caught up later, then he would have to face the music again. So Darren decided to tell all about his rampage of burglary and asked for the ninety-eight others to be taken into account. It is likely the police would never have solved the ninety-eight crimes; it certainly aided the crime clear-up rate.

The police did not close the file once he had been sentenced and returned to Borstal. They wanted to learn what had happened to the property. In all, Darren had stolen about £15,000 worth of goods. He was likely to have been paid about £5000 cash by receivers. But he certainly was not telling. The police knew he had lied about this when they questioned him about disposal after he confessed to the other ninety-eight crimes.

In Darren's code of conduct there was something to be gained by confessing to the crimes – he did not have to worry about being caught for them later. The bonus was that he could wipe his slate clean without suffering. He was going back to Borstal anyway. He declared to the court that all the proceeds of crime had been spent. The police had to admit that, when his flat was searched, all they could find was £100. The magistrates had ordered that sum to be paid in compensation.

The police were far from satisfied. They searched and found his address-book. One of his 'friends', Tony, was a suspected receiver. The local detective inspector made up a raiding party and obtained a search warrant.

Tony lived in a detached bungalow in Finsbury. Two detectives were detailed to watch the rear in case Tony tried to flee. When the inspector knocked at the front door, other officers were already at the side-door. But the inspector knew from experience that he had been beaten the moment Tony opened the door. Tony glanced at the warrant authorising a search and spread open his hands. 'Come on in, Guv, there's nothing here.' A long search proved fruitless. As an experienced 'fence' (a dealer in the proceeds of crime) Tony knew he would be visited by the law from the moment he heard of Darren's arrest. He had made trebly sure that not one item in his house could be identified as the proceeds of crime.

The police departed an hour later empty-handed. Police work is often frustrating. But the inspector did not give up. He contacted the Borstal housing Darren, and asked to be kept informed of the identities and addresses of all visitors Darren received. As the names came into the police, as the weeks rolled by, so they were listed by the 'intelligence collator'. Each name was put on the index and cross-related to Darren. The police were confident this would pay dividends in the years ahead.

For Darren, the next year consisted of study – the more he learned about antiques, the better. He had been taught a useful profession. He had realised the importance during his burglary spree. Buyers of antiques knew what they were about, so it was vital, if a burglar were to receive a fair deal, that he, too, knew the trade. Darren decided that it would pay handsomely if, at the Government's expense, he learned a really useful trade.

Nine months later he was free again. He had spent his eighteenth birthday inside and he was determined to make up for lost time. His biggest and most immediate problem was getting started again. He had to prepare himself properly before hitting the trail. He had no intention this time of rushing in and getting caught. He needed some equipment and good information, and this called for ready cash. One thing was sure: Darren had many friends. These included 'dippers' – a team of pickpockets and purse snatchers.

It was June and the tourist season was in full swing with plenty of money readily available for the enterprising teams. 'Dipping' has its attractions – often, if the victim is a tourist, he returns home and the chances of being identified are reduced. This time, Darren decided to move into the Manor Park, Tottenham area on the north side of the Thames.

It was six weeks before the Yard's Flying Squad unit specialising in 'dips' spotted Darren. They followed him for an hour, but he soon had that uncomfortable feeling that the law was close. Eventually, the Flying Squad confronted Darren. There was no evidence against him. The only gain was the intelligence, so the report that he was now 'working' in Tottenham was duly recorded in the intelligence files. An added memo stated the police guessed his work was 'dipping'.

The 'dipping' soon served Darren's purpose. A friend had a car and was keen to team up. Darren was back in business, and determined to make burglary pay.

He lasted two months before being arrested again. The night

before, he had pulled a good job in Kent – a nice country house in a nice village. He had gone for the antiques. There had been a good grandfather clock in the hall, obviously the owner's pride and joy. They had gained access through a side-window, and the car had been backed up into the empty garage. Darren held a pencil torch in his gloved hands and was admiring the clock when his Borstal training really paid off. He had opened the door in the front of the clock to check the markings. There were none. The clock was a fake – a skilful reproduction. The owner had been taken for an expensive ride at a sale. If Darren had not learned his trade, he, too, would have been a victim of a faker and the whole night's work would have been wasted.

Darren was furious. He turned his attention to the rest of the house. In the study his luck changed. There, in a corner, was a small steel safe. It was certainly heavy. However, it could be moved because it was not bolted to the floor or cemented to the wall. Darren was not a safe breaker by trade. It had to be removed. He could not open it on the spot. What the haul would turn out to be would have to wait until the morning. The first vital act was to remove the safe from the premises. The operation went well. When the house-owner returned, Darren was asleep in London with the safe locked in the boot of the car.

In the morning, fresh from a deep sleep, Darren's first thoughts were about the safe. What riches did it contain? He had no idea at that moment that behind the steel door of the small safe was £4000 in notes – cash which the owner was reluctant to bank because of the risk of the taxman asking questions. Darren and his accomplice met soon after breakfast and drove to the yard of a south-east London salvage firm. The firm was known to both burglars and police as a thieves' swap shop, a place where all types of dubious transactions took place without any awkward questions – subject to payment of an appropriate fee. Because the firm dealt in salvage – from fires, car accidents or burst water-pipes – it quite legally had the equipment Darren required: oxyacetylene cutters. A quick word with the 'manager' of the day, and a promise of a 'good drink' if there were valuables inside, and the metal cutting torch was in action.

Two detectives on surveillance duty on the roof of a high-rise block a quarter of a mile away had a good bird's-eye view of the action in the yard through their binoculars. It was a secret lookout post often used and it paid off regular dividends. Those arrested in the salvage yard had not worked out where the law was getting its information from; the obvious explanation was that the police had tailed suspects and just moved in. In reality, it was not that haphazard. The officers on the rooftop used their personal radio to alert the cruising 'Q' car not far away. Darren and his associate were so engrossed in their job that the 'Q' car was well into the yard before they saw the danger.

No question of taking the safe with them now; it was their own skins they had to save as they bolted. Darren leapt over a wall and into the entrance of the first block of flats. He was wearing a distinctive blue-and-white-striped, open-necked shirt and a blazer. He ripped off the shirt and then decided to take a chance. He walked boldly out into the street. His freedom lasted only another sixty seconds because, at that moment, the 'Q' car hunting the men from the yard turned into the road. Darren's accomplice was never caught – and Darren gave no help. The crime had been committed in Kent, so Darren was taken under escort by the Metropolitan Police and handed over to an officer of the local force at Maidstone.

He was in court next day, and an application for bail was granted by the magistrates. Darren's solicitor told the court no violence had been used – Darren had not assaulted the police during arrest. The case was eventually to be heard at a Kent Crown Court in April 1976, but that was seven months away. Darren appreciated there was a risk that when the case was eventually heard he might be sent to prison. He would then be nineteen.

So it was back to work. Precisely how many crimes Darren successfully carried out is not known. The police can only surmise. Exactly a week after he was bailed, a south London pub, of which Darren was a regular customer, was burgled. The safe went, containing £7000. Again, the cash had been kept on the premises by a landlord not wishing to let the taxman know of the undeclared profits from the snack bar. Darren was arrested as a suspect. But this time there was no evidence: there was no trace of the safe.

Two months later, the police were again looking for Darren as a suspect. A country mansion in Gloucestershire had been burgled. About £20,000 worth of silverware had been stolen. There were no clues at the house, but an early-morning newspaper delivery-boy had spotted two men driving away. The description of one of the men in the car matched Darren. Again, Darren was located and questioned. Again, no clues or evidence – only suspicions.

All the officers who had dealt with Darren before were alerted by the Yard's CID. Regular sighting reports flowed in. Darren was clearly successful. He was now often spotted in expensive cars, with girls driving. The ownership of each vehicle was checked. It was soon clear that Darren had a new steady girlfriend, the daughter of a successful Kent farmer. Yvonne even drove him to the police station – a condition of his bail was that he report once a week. Police, as a matter of routine, noted who was with Darren each time – identification was made easy because the girl drove a new Rover car registered in her name. Darren was also spending considerably. He was not working, and he spent most of his days and nights in pubs and clubs.

Darren had certainly changed one of his ways: he was avoiding either driving or travelling in stolen cars. The police realised this as soon as Yvonne stopped acting as his driver. She vanished from the scene after three months. Maybe his money had run out, or the girl had learned too much about her boyfriend. Anyway, Darren had a new form of transport – minicabs – always hired from the same firm in Tooting, London.

At last the day of reckoning for the £4000 safe-burglary came up. Darren could do little else but plead guilty – he had been caught red-handed, so there was little point in arguing the case. Darren's logical mind also figured that the judge might be more lenient in an undefended case because it did not waste the court's time. The police noted the sentence without enthusiasm. Two years' imprisonment suspended for two years. This meant that, if Darren could keep out of court for the next twenty-four months, the sentence would expire. If he was convicted, he would have to serve the two years in jail – on top of whatever sentence the new court imposed. In addition, he was placed under a supervision order for two years. Then came the sting: he was ordered to pay £25 compensation to the owner of the safe for damage done in breaking in, plus a £200 fine with six months' imprisonment in default of payment.

A relieved Darren was delighted. 'Time to pay the fine, Your Honour?' he asked. The judge was told that Darren was unemployed. 'Five pounds a week until the £200 is paid in full,' came the order. Darren walked free. Life was picking up.

It was time for celebrating. It was the rounds of the clubs and pubs to toast his freedom. Two days after sentence, at 2.00 a.m., Darren had a fresh brush with the law. He was a passenger in a car driven by a 'business friend' returning home across south London. The car was being driven rather erratically. The police stopped the car and asked the driver to undergo the breath test. Now, Darren did not think much of this. He began to tell the officer what he thought of the law. Darren's views were not welcome and he was arrested for interfering.

The police used this minor incident to update their intelligence on Darren. His address, given in the sober light of day, turned out to be that of a woman whose husband was at present in jail for burglary. Darren admitted that he lived with her 'on and off'. Pressed about the source of his money, he gave details of public houses in which he claimed he worked as a part-time barman.

Three months later he was arrested again, this time on the Sussex coast. It was the usual story – burglary of a house, obtaining property by deception. One item he had stolen was a wallet with credit cards which he had used.

Now Darren had to pay. The two years' suspended was now enforced because Darren had been convicted. In all, he received a total of three years in a proper jail.

As all criminals know today, three years in jail does not really mean three years in jail. In Darren's case it was, in fact, twelve months before he was allowed early release on parole on condition that he returned home.

Christmas 1977 and the New Year came and went happily, but our Darren was changing. He was now just twenty and he decided on a change of appearance. He purchased a pair of spectacles with thick black frames. The lenses were grey-tinted, and his hair had been streaked with grey. He looked older than his twenty years.

How the police learned this latest snippet was not accidental. A small team of burglars had been arrested and were on trial at a London Crown Court. Detectives were noting faces in the public gallery as evidence was being given. Who should be there but Darren. The spectacles and hair initially puzzled the detectives, but after a few discreet questions his identity was confirmed.

Three months later, the appearance changed yet again – Darren had a complete perm. He changed his whole style of dress. Police were finding it harder to keep track of him. Darren was no longer the juvenile who was so easy to detect and arrest. Eleven years in the burglary business had taught him many lessons.

Darren has now graduated into professional crime. It has provided him with an attractive living. The penalties he has had to pay along the way have been in reality minor. The periods during which he was removed from society were brief. His biggest set-back now is that he is a marked man. The police have his fingerprints. They have a bulging criminal record file on him. In addition, the police know of his associates, his haunts, his habits – even the latest dodge of disguising himself.

Darren's case-history may, on the face of it, seem remarkable. But experienced police officers insist that in the burglary business there are many thousands like Darren. Darren's history has been relatively easy to chart, only because he has fallen into the hands of the police and the courts so often. At each court-hearing Darren is reminded of his criminal past because it is submitted to the magistrates or judge to help in the considerations regarding punishment.

Has Darren reformed? What of his future? There are no indications that Darren has the slightest intention of turning away from crime, nor from burglary in particular. He enters the eighties as chief suspect in a new police investigation. Burglary, naturally.

The Evidence

Here is the proof of the astonishing judicial leniency towards burglars. These are re-creations of the official criminal record sheets produced in open court each time a burglar is convicted.

The first evidence of the policy which does so little to deter burglars is in Darren's record sheet. Despite a shocking record, magistrates in three separate cases – all within three months – imposed suspended sentences.

METROPOLITAN POLICE

Convictions recorded against: DARREN   Criminal Record......
                                                Office No. ....

Date	Offences (with details of any offence taken into consideration)	Sentence	Date of release
1968	Housebreaking and stealing	Conditional discharge for 12 months	
1970	Burglary	Probation for 2 years	
1970	Theft of 2 toolsets	Attendance centre for 12 hours	
1970	(1) Attempted burglary	(1) Conditional discharge for 9 months	
	(2) Burglary (original offence earlier in 1970)	(2) Attendance centre for 12 hours	
1970	(1) Taking and driving away (2) No insurance (3) Driving while disqualified because of age	(1–3) Conditional discharge for 12 months	
1970	Theft of money from coin-box (12s)	Sent to approved school	
1971	(1) Burglary (2) Allowing himself to be carried (12 cases to be considered)	(1–2) 3 months' detention	1971
1972	Committing an act with intent to impede the apprehension and prosecution of an offender	Fined £5	
1972	Possessing an offensive weapon	Bound over for sum of £25 for 12 months	
1973	Handling stolen goods	Fined £5	
1973	Burglary	Detention centre for 6 months	1974
1973	(1) Taking and driving away (2) No insurance (3) Driving while disqualified	(1–3) Fined £5 or 1 day on each case. Disqualified for 2 years on (1)	

1973	(1) Driving while disqualified (2) Taking and driving away (3) No insurance	(1–3) Absolute discharge

1973	(1) Taking and driving away
	
	(2) No insurance
		(1) Fined £15 or 1 day
		    police detention
		(2) Fined £15 or 1 day
		    police detention

1973	(1) Driving while disqualified (2) Taking and driving away (3) No insurance	(1–3) Absolute discharge in each case
1973	(1) Theft of meat from warehouse where employed (2) Taking and driving away	(1–2) Borstal training

1974	(1) Burglary
	(2) Driving while disqualified
	(3) Attempted burglary
	(4) Burglary
	(5) Allowing himself to be carried
	(6) Burglary
	(7) Burglary
	98 cases considered: theft (5);
	    burglary (72); taking and driving
	    away (18); attempted taking and
	    driving away (1); alleged burglary
	    (2)
		(1, 3, 4, 6) Borstal training
		(2 and 5) 1 day's jail on
		    each case
		Pay £103
		
		(7) Borstal training

1976	Attempted taking and driving away	6 weeks' jail, suspended for 2 years Disqualified for 2 months Pay £30 Legal Aid
1976	Burglary	18 months' jail, suspended for 2 years

1976	Burglary	2 years' jail, suspended for
		    2 years, and suspended
		    sentence supervision
		    order for 2 years
		Disqualified 5 years
		Pay £25 compensation
		Fined £200 or 6 months'
		    jail

1976	(1 and 3) Burglary (2 cases)
	(4) Burglary (i.e., suspended
	    sentence, offence of earlier 1976)
	(5) Burglary (suspended sentence
	    offence of earlier 1976)
	
	(5 cases of obtaining property by
	    deception considered)
		(1) 30 months' jail
		(2) 3 months' jail
		(3) 6 months' jail
		
		(2) 3 months' jail
		(4) 18 months' jail
		(5) 2 years' jail

1977	Theft of wallet containing £4
	(4 cases of handling stolen goods
	    considered)
		12 months' jail,
		    concurrent with present
		    sentence

To prove that Darren is no exception, here is a re-creation of the criminal record sheet of a provincial burglar. It proves that once on the burglary trail it is hard to get off.

Nick's first conviction in the north of England was in 1940. Thirty-nine years later, he was again celebrating the new year with another appearance – his twenty-third hearing.

Sentencing for burglary varies nationwide – Nick's punishments appear slightly harsher than Darren's, who operated in the south. But in nearly every burglary case the punishment is very weak – not really a deterrent to a persistent offender. Remember also that the courts' verdicts that make up the criminal record sheets are only for the offences for which the criminal is 'captured' or opts to confess to the police.

Nick's history of crime, which began at the end of the Second World War, is similar to Darren's. Here is the evidence:

COUNTY CONSTABULARY

Convictions recorded against: NICK

Criminal record........
Office No. ....

Date	Offences (with details of any offence taken into consideration	Sentence	Date of release
1940	Shopbreaking and larceny, stealing from unattended vehicle	Probation, 12 months	
1940	Stealing cycle (5 offences considered)	Bound over £5 for 12 months	
1940	Stealing cycle	Sent to an approved school	
1945	Larceny (2 cases) (8 offences taken into consideration)	Sent to an approved school	
1947	Stealing money from offertory box (8 offences considered)	Bound over £5 for 12 months	
1948	Stealing overcoat from unattended vehicle (2 offences taken into consideration)	3 years Borstal training	1950
1951	Stealing money from church	18 months' jail	1952
1952	Housebreaking and stealing money from meter	21 months' jail	
1953	Stealing pedal cycle Attempted larceny from church box	3 and 3 years' jail	1955
1955	Sacrilege and larceny Housebreaking and larceny (16 offences taken into account)	2½, 2½ and 2½ years' jail	1957
1957	Stealing 6s 9d from public toilet Stealing pedal cycle	3 months and 3 months	1957

1957	Taking and driving away No insurance No driving licence	3 months' jail concurrent with earlier 1957 conviction Disqualified for 6 months No separate penalty imposed	
1958	Attempted stealing from church offertory box	12 months' jail	
1960	Housebreaking and stealing (2 cases) (9 cases breaking and stealing, 1 case larceny taken into account)	7 years' preventive detention	1964
1965	(1) Housebreaking and stealing (2) Housebreaking and stealing (3) Shopbreaking and stealing (4) Sacrilege (5) Housebreaking and stealing	(1–5) Probation 3 years 3 years with condition of residence	
1965	(1) Stealing first-aid box and contents (2) Attempted housebreaking (3) Housebreaking and stealing (4) Housebreaking and stealing	8 years' preventive detention on each, to run concurrently Order of £100 compensation	
1970	Burglary	4 years' jail (extended sentence) consecutive to present sentence	
1970	Appeal Court	Varied on appeal to 2 years' jail from 1970	
1972	(1) Burglary (2) Burglary	(1–3) 3 years' jail on each case	1973
1974	(1–3) Burglary (2 cases) (2) Theft from car (4) Theft from house (8) cases considered, i.e., 1 theft; 5 burglaries; 1 attempted burglary; 1 pecuniary advantage)	(1–4) 2 years' jail on each case	1975
1975	(1) Burglary (2) Forgery (3) Endeavouring to obtain property by forged instrument (4) Burglary (2 cases considered, 1 forgery; 1 burglary and theft)	(1–4) Sentence deferred until 1976 but 5 years' jail on each case in 1975	
1975	(1–2) Burglary (3) Taking and driving away (4) Burglary (15 cases considered, 4 taking and driving away; 4 burglary and theft; 1 attempted burglary; 2 pecuniary advantage by deception)	(1, 2, 4) 5 years' jail on each case (3) 12 months' jail	1979

1979	(1) Taking and driving away	(1) Fined £75 and licence endorsed
	(2) No insurance	(2) Fined £25 and licence endorsed
	(3) No MoT	(3) Fined £5

3 Burglars at Work

Every type of individual can be found in the ranks of the burglars. Most are totally heartless, simply bent on taking any item of property belonging to another for their own profit.

For example, Alan had already purchased a gold ring for his marriage to Valerie when the burglar came to his south Croydon home. Not content with ransacking the house for family heirlooms, the burglar also took the wedding-ring despite the fact that, clearly, a wedding was imminent. Nothing is really sacred. It is just a question of supplying items demanded by receivers who have clients.

Burglars undoubtedly get tall orders from their distributors, but they usually oblige – even when a five-foot-long Royal African python is top of the order-book. A brown eighteen-month-old reptile, valued at £37, was located and stolen. The victim, a Croydon pet-shop owner, explained: 'A whole lot of people keep snakes – more than most people realise. There is a demand for snakes, scorpions, tarantulas; but whoever stole the python knew exactly where to go. It was not poisonous. It kills through strangulation, but I don't think it would hurt a man – even if he was a burglar.'

Even the dead are not immune. A middle-aged, well-dressed man apparently in deep mourning – he was clad in a dark suit and a black tie – called on a south London antique-dealer and asked for help. The caller said his aunt had died and it was his duty to clear out the contents of her house. Would the dealer be interested? An appointment to view the house was made. When the dealer arrived a few hours later at the Dulwich house the man in mourning answered his knock. Offers for various items of furniture were made and accepted, and £700 in cash changed hands.

The man in mourning then said he must leave the dealer to load up, because he had to go and see other relatives about the sale. He promised to be back shortly. The dealer eventually grew tired of waiting and shut the door, leaving a note saying that if any more items were for sale he would be interested. The note was found by genuine relatives a few days later. The 'mourner' was a burglar who, on finding the house empty with only heavy items of furniture of value still there, decided to cash in by a confidence trick.

Even though they are burglars, and therefore criminals, some have a perverted sense of humour. One burglar who broke into a home in Romford, Essex, helped himself to a big meal, in payment for which he left behind a diamond ring stolen from another house.

A Harrogate business executive returned home from an overseas trip to find his store of drinks had been raided. In exchange the burglar had left behind four oil paintings from another raid.

In Folkestone a raider broke into a house and found the occupier, a ninety-two-year-old woman, on the floor, helpless after a fall several hours earlier. He helped her on to the bed, explained that he still had to steal because he was desperate, and left with £16 in cash after kissing his victim.

The Informants

Liz, at twenty-eight, would have graced the cover of any pin-up magazine or newspaper. She was dressed as a model and displayed the same confidence. In fact the large woollen bag which she carried stamped her as one of the many dozens of girls hired each day by photographers from the highly reputable agencies that supply models to sport the fashions for the next season.

Liz had in fact come from an agency when she made straight for the lift to take her to a room in a Mayfair hotel. She made a very good living working as a masseuse. Her rounds were the apartments of good hotels, fashionable town flats and the big houses.

The glossy girlie magazines are packed with advertisements from agencies that supply girls like Liz. The routine line is: 'After your busy business day relax in the comfort and privacy of your home, flat, or hotel room with a delightful masseuse who will ease the cares of the world away. . . .' There is a big demand for these girls who offer 'complete body massage'. Some are in fact genuine and highly professional, but many operate using the profession of masseuse as a thinly disguised cover for prostitution. The girls, who advertise themselves as being intelligent and beautiful, make a basic charge of £17.50 to £25 for 'delightful and exotic full body massage'. The customer also has to pay the girl's return taxi-fare. On arrival at a house, flat or hotel room, the girl is always careful not to make a blatant sex-offer – in case the 'customer' is a police officer and the visit is a trap. But once the customer is aroused during the massage the girls who are in the game for the big money for sex expertly steer the conversation round to the real subject. A further payment buys sex, the fee depending on the type of sex service.

What sexual activities go on between a customer and a girl is a matter between them only. But a large portion of the 'straight fee' for the massage is payable after the visit by the girl to the agency. The agency works for the money. Men responding to the advertisements are fixed with appointments and given the details of the girl who will be sent. A phone number is always requested by the agency – for the staff make a return call to check that the man making the booking is genuine and not a phoney.

This army of girls touring the bedrooms of men who have money has not gone unnoticed by the men in the burglary business. They have recruited from among the ranks of the massage girls, making handsome payments for information and help. Sometimes the girls are simply asked to note the type of security inside the house, and where the valuables are located. Others are paid larger fees to play a more active role.

One dodge is for a girl who draws a very wealthy 'punter', as the clients are usually called, to go far beyond the normal services. Often the man is lonely and, after a massage and sex, is delighted to find his companion attractive, and she is willing to go out for a drink or a meal. While the girl keeps the client occupied eating or drinking away from the hotel room, flat or house, the burglars move in, knowing that they will not be disturbed. The girl could hardly be accused of the burglary when it is later discovered; she has a perfect alibi, from the client she has accompanied.

The number of girls on the massage trail who have links with crime syndicates is now causing grave concern to Scotland Yard. It is hard for the police to get across the message to wealthy businessmen that inviting a strange girl into their bedroom leaves them exposed to a real risk of robbery. Some girls are known to have developed the art of never quite shutting the entrance-door properly after their arrival. It is all too easy for burglars to slip in and do their business while the man who is being robbed enjoys a massage in the shower, bath or bed, oblivious to the action in other rooms.

It is not only girls on the sex circuit who are used by burglars. The professional burglars are opportunists, anxious to glean information from any person with inside knowledge. It is the same story with bank robberies: bank clerks have been sought out by gangs for office secrets. It is a similar story with big-time burglars. Staff, particularly girls, employed in estate agencies are always a target for the gangs. A seduced secretary in an estate agent's office has the opportunity to borrow keys to the bigger properties and flats, enabling her burglar-boyfriend to make copies for later use.

The girl on the front step was tall, had a stunning figure, and her two-piece suit was the latest fashion. Under her unbuttoned jacket was a white, open-necked silk shirt. One of the first impressions the occupant who opened his front door had was that the girl was not wearing a bra under the shirt.

'I am a member of a team in this area and we are conducting research to establish what social amenities are most wanted,' said the girl.

The occupant, Philip, had been retired three years. He was at home alone. His wife had just gone shopping. The girl carried a clipboard. She flipped over the first sheet of paper and asked if Philip would assist her by answering questions. It was an April morning, but a chilling wind blew on the doorstep.

Philip agreed and invited the girl in. She was charm itself, very disarming, and the questions she asked seemed authentic enough. How long would the wife be out? She would like to have her views as well. Not long, said Philip, and the girl graciously accepted an offer of a cup of tea. The brew-up in the kitchen only took a few minutes. On his return to the lounge the tea was hurriedly drunk and the girl apologised for not being able to stay longer. She would try to call back to see the wife later. A friendly handshake on the doormat and a wave goodbye.

The wife had hardly been back a few minutes when the girl researcher returned. This time she was accompanied by a colleague, whom she said had finished his interview. Both were admitted this time. As the wife answered the girl's questions her colleague interrupted. A call of nature – could he pop out and use the toilet? He was directed to the small room 'up the stairs and immediately on the left'. The girl continued her questioning. A few minutes later the man returned to the session in the lounge. The work completed, there were more thanks, and a final goodbye.

It was not until two hours later, when the wife walked into her bedroom, that she realised something was wrong. The bed had been disturbed. They were lucky. Their small saving had not been kept under the mattress. But the holiday savings in the pot on top of the wardrobe had gone. So, too, had her few pieces of jewellery. Not a big haul – £270 in cash and rings and a necklace, irreplaceable as personal items, but having a face value on the secondhand market of £1500. Not a killing financially for the two 'researchers', but they had succeeded in five other homes in the area. By the evening the local police estimated the couple had raised about £7000 that morning. By the time the police alerted the local officers to watch for the couple, they were far away – selecting a new area for the next 'hit'.

In the burglary business not all thieves operate by breaking into unoccupied homes. There are many refinements. Good burglars are opportunists. How better to evaluate a house or a flat as a target than simply to walk up to the front door and knock?

Every day there is an army of genuine callers, knocking at doors all over the country. Among the ranks of the doorstep salesmen and researchers are the professional burglars. Many doorstep salesmen and women are, of course, genuine. And some who are not what they claim to be are not always burglars. The man posing as an 'educational researcher' may simply be a slick salesman for encyclopedias. The man selling items for the 'blind' and 'disabled' may just be selling to line his own pockets. The man who calls saying he can help cut the fuel bills may really be a central-heating salesman. The man who flashes the big card marked 'security' may really be a genuine representative for a firm selling anti-burglar devices.

However, the stark fact is that nearly always the callers are total strangers. Police investigations into burglars have proved that among that army of front-door callers are both burglars and 'spies' for the burglary gangs. So often the activities of a sales group in a district are followed within days by a rash of burglaries. For it is very simple for a salesman to note mentally the type of security devices – or lack of them.

Clearly, all salesmen and researchers cannot be banned. It would not be desirable or possible in a free society. But there are some answers. These range from simply saying, 'Not today, thank you,' to taking the sensible precaution of asking for proof of identification. The Market Research Society, for example, has faced up to this problem for the 184 research organisations based in London. Initially, their members wanted action taken to hit what the trade calls 'suggers' – those who sell under the guise of being market researchers.

Genuine market research enquiries carried out by trained doorstep and street interviewers can benefit both the informant and the companies commissioning the surveys. Suggers and burglars who pose as research interviewers do the profession no good. So now genuine market researchers are being issued with identity cards carrying a picture of the holder, with telephone numbers and details of the organisation they represent, so that anyone in doubt can make a check call.

The Rolls-Royce Burglars

They were young, good-looking, expensively dressed and had all the trappings of wealth. And they travelled everywhere by Rolls-Royce.

The façade was procured from the proceeds of other people's hard work. The Rolls had been selected only because it jointly provided first-class 'cover' and, more practically, had a huge boot.

The young men, in their twenties, were the new breed of super-burglars. They were making a fortune from the modern phenomenon of robbing other people's homes with impunity. Through the generations society has always harboured their type – people who see and grasp the opportunity of getting rich quick, because they find and exploit a chink in modern society's armour: too few police are tackling too much crime, leaving the personal possessions of workers of every class vulnerable to the 'help-yourself brigade'.

But these burglars – typical of so many of the teams working the urban residential areas today – were not after the small fry. They pitched their play with the same expertise as any professional marketing agency. Their target was the upper-middle-class home-stead – not too VIP (such as Ministers or showbiz stars), that would attract too much publicity. They made a mistake occasionally by hitting the home of some newsworthy person who generated such media attention that the local police *had* to put up a good public show by responding with much apparent activity against the law-breakers. But everyone makes mistakes. No, the people this team went for were the families who were successful and had all the affluence of modern society: the videotape recorders, the chain saws, the portable televisions in the children's bedroom, the family silver, the minks – all the articles so easily saleable with so few questions asked.

They view the occasional penalty just as a junior executive with a parking-ticket on the company car owned by a firm that declines as a matter of principle to be responsible for the fines: he pays it out of 'expenses'. The occasional arrest was a painless occupational hazard that could be dealt with out of profits. But they were professional. They did not get the Rolls, the handsome bank account, the homes packed full of other people's valuables without being good at their job.

These two burglars had a strict routine. Top priority was given to daily physical exercise. Together, most days, they would jog and sprint on alternate laps around their local park. They sweated and toiled – but a job with rich returns warranted the effort. The real work came between 11.00 a.m. and 3.00 p.m., crucial times for the professional. Experience has shown that during these four hours a home is most vulnerable.

They were versatile regarding their target areas. The two-man team (whose activities I have studied in depth and whose deeds I relate here) had a large 'manor'. It began in the prosperous area

St John's Wood, of London, through West Hampstead, Finchley, Whetstone and Barnet, then on through Mill Hill, Harrow, down to Ealing, and across the Thames into Putney and Walton-on-Thames. In a good week they could successfully burglarise forty properties.

Dress was vital. Smart but not flashy – nothing to attract attention, nothing that a witness could definitely recall. Suits only. Who, in a Rolls, ever carried a mackintosh? Most important, a mac or a brolly would be a hindrance if, despite the best-laid plans, they had to sprint to freedom.

Shoes were their weak point. The average detective has leather-soled shoes which are slippery in a tight corner. Officers who opt for rubber do not fare too well, either, when it is a hard turn on wet grass. But track shoes are often worn by burglars – many a break-in man's downfall, but the pros outnumber the cons.

Frank and Miles, twenty-four and thirty-four respectively, had it all worked out. They drove into the district selected as starting-point for the day's activities, never parking in the road of the target house but leaving the 'wheels' around the first corner. One well-favoured method was for Miles to walk boldly up to the front door and ring the bell. Meanwhile, Frank leaped over the garden wall to seek an access point. Miles continued ringing. His hope was that when the door was opened the person on the other side would be Frank.

Once inside, every second is vital. Good burglars are like magpies – they take everything, even the jar of instant coffee. After all, it costs over a pound a go. More important, from a professional burglar's point of view, a jar of coffee, or a box of washing-powder, is unlikely to be listed on police files. They are untraceable – and the burglar's own wife or girlfriend faces the same high shopping-bills as anyone else.

The getaway is the riskiest part, but cheek and bluff are part of the burglar's stock in trade. Favourite 'exits' of Frank and Miles included brazenly walking out of the front door with suitcases packed full of silver, the husband's golf clubs over the shoulder, and a cheerful word for any passer-by.

Back in the Rolls, it was away home for a share-out. There is a huge market waiting to buy. Stolen goods do not remain in the hands of the burglar for long. After the hi-fis, the tape recorders, the jewellery, the credit cards, cheque-books, cash and the more obvious items have been sorted out, there always remains a collection of leftovers. Good professionals lump these assortments into a suitcase kept just for this purpose. And they sell them off as special 'job lots' to auctioneers.

The Story of David

Burglary is the spawning-ground which breeds criminals, who graduate into other spheres of crime.

David, now thirty-eight, has graduated from burglary with a knowledgeable degree in practices of the underworld that well qualifies him for his work as an international criminal. He is now into white-collar crime or, more simply, fraud on a grand scale. He has accounts in many banks in many towns and in many names. He lives by his wits and, for the most part, is successful. His income is often large – but so are his expenses. When David is in the money it is first-class all the way – and all the way is often a tour of the world's top playgrounds with a beautiful girl. He has never had any shortage of beautiful girls willing to accompany him on play trips that last up to six months. They remain as long as the cash and the credit cards (which enable him to sign bills for travel and hotels which he seldom settles) last.

David is no stranger to prison, and there are several countries where he is *persona non grata*. He refers to these countries as having 'capital punishment'. In his book it means: 'If you have capital, you don't get punished.'

I have monitored David's career for many years. I believe he is typical of the youngster who leaves school at the earliest opportunity, turns to burglary for a living, and then switches to hard-to trace crimes, such as fraud.

I recently met David again, following his latest deportation – this time from the United States. The American immigration authorities decided he was undesirable even as a visitor because they found him travelling with bank accounts and papers under a series of aliases, while his genuine passport and papers were locked up in a safe-deposit box hundreds of miles away.

Younger friends, still in the burglary game, hold David as a nice-type hero. They are even lending part of the cash proceeds of crime to him, confident that he will soon be flush again and repay handsomely.

Over a pub lunch I asked David to undergo a bit of self-analysis. How had he first gone into burglary? What lessons, if any, had he learned from his experiences? With what I accepted as sincerity he said: 'If I could start my life again, I would try to educate myself a lot better. That's my biggest regret. I went to secondary school and couldn't wait to leave at fifteen. My dad wanted me to get a trade. All I wanted to do was to get out of school. So I agreed to go to a technical school. That got me signed off from school. I only stayed at the tech one week. I wanted to get the same big money as my mates.

I was finished with pocket money. So I left and joined my pals. They were all at it – burglary appeared so easy then. We had it all worked out. You only needed to work for a brief period each day. We knew that the police shifts change over at 10.00 p.m. Well, the cops that are finishing have to get back to the station, don't they? And the new shift doesn't go out early. So that was the time to hit – between 9.50 and 10.00 p.m.

'We would do the research during the day. It was mainly shops. You could wander in during the day as a customer. You would look for the bolts and the alarms and what was best to take. You only go for the saleable goods – cigarettes, spirits in off-licences, and carpets. Never any trouble with things like that. Anything people use you can sell. OK, you only get a third of the proper price. But if you were offered a bottle of gin today at a third the cost would you say no?

'All sounds great, but really it was harder than working at a regular job. You would meet in the morning about nine o'clock and decide where to look. And it would be midnight before you were home. OK, there was plenty of time to spend in the pubs. But it was hard graft really. And I got caught a couple of times. I realised then that I would eventually get bird [jail] if I carried on. So I took a job in a scrap-metal yard. I enjoyed that. Then a bird [girlfriend] came along. And I got her in the family way. We married, and do you know what happened? She wanted me home all the time. That may be all right, but if you are at home a lot of time you can't earn money. So I went back to the boys after the baby was born.

'I wanted money, so we worked the East End – I was living south of the river then. It was easy. We'd kick a door in or crowbar it open and have whatever we wanted away.

'You know, I used to take that risk for a few quid. Now, I wouldn't even listen to a job unless there was at least five grand [£5000] in it for me. Anyway, I wanted to get back into the scrap-metal business.

'When I got £600 saved up from screwing [burglary] I bought a tipper truck. Well, the £600 was the deposit. It really cost £3000 and I had it on HP. I'd go anywhere. I was working for myself, and it was good.

'I'd take iron to Nottingham and bring a load of coal back. Anything that was business. All I was doing was work. But I had a real incentive. Then my luck ran out. I was coming back from Rugby in my tipper and I had only had three hours' sleep in the last twenty-four. What happened? I fell asleep at the wheel and wrecked the truck and nearly myself as well. I had insurance, but it was going to be at least six months before it could be settled by the insurance people, repaired and back on the road.

48

'I still had to pay the HP. I was soon in debt. A scrap-metal pal of mine said he would take over the HP payments and I could repay him later. What with two lots of interest, I was being sucked under. So I told the scrap-metal dealer, after a few weeks, that he could keep the truck in settlement of everything and I was out.

'I had heard of a better scheme – screwing golf clubhouses. Driving my truck I had used maps and had noted that among the many things they list are golf clubs. Now, golf clubhouses have bottles of booze, cigarette-machines and one-armed bandits. So I palled up with a mate who had a motor. By day we would drive around to the golf courses shown on the maps. What we wanted were the ones which were non-residential. You could easily see if the club had a steward living in, or a resident professional. We did well. One-armed bandits became our speciality. We used to take the cash and resell the machine for £100 a time. There was no shortage of takers.

'If there was an alarm, we used to pour in plaster of Paris to freeze it. Alarms were not as good as they are now. You wouldn't get away with it now. But even then we had one big shock. We had immobilised an alarm at a clubhouse and in we went. But no sooner had we forced the door than the whole place was bathed in floodlights. They had linked the alarm to the floodlights. Although the bell could not ring, it had not stopped the lights being switched on. It was like midday rather than midnight. We didn't hang around.

'That was when I finally quit burglary. The police had raided a pub for opening after hours. In the pub was one of my one-armed bandits. The cops asked the landlord where he had got it. He grassed on me, and I was nicked. I got six months – and I saw the warning lights. There is no big money in burglary – yes, a few thousand here and there, but it's hard work. You could make more going legitimate.

'So I switched to more intelligent things – the tourist trade. I became a guide first and then linked up with a pal, running a limousine-hire service for tourists. The Americans were always wanting to buy cars – Rolls, old cars, all that sort of thing. Well, we'd agree to ship them back out after the tourists had gone. What really happened was, we'd say there was a delay and use the motor to take other tourists around. They would get the car, all right, in the end – but not before we had months of free use. More intelligent than burglary. Now I'm into something new. Like the car caper, it's not really criminal. That's for the boys.'

Like the professional crook he is, David declines to talk about his more current white-collar crimes. He has learned from his burglary days that that is a risk not worth taking.

The Cat Burglars

Burglars come in all types, shapes, forms and guises. The professionals operating in small teams opt for the straightforward approach – the knock on the door to see if anyone is at home, the forced lock or broken window to gain entry – but there is no thief so specialised as the cat burglar. The very name suggests agility, climbing powers, speed, stealth.

Arthur, a thirty-four-year-old casual labourer, had all these attributes. He became a cat burglar not only to make money; he also wanted excitement. It was a perversion. The dizzy heights, the physical demands – barring the odd accident, of course – gave Arthur job satisfaction. A suspended jail sentence following a job that went wrong was no deterrent to him. It acted as an aphrodisiac. When he launched his latest war on society in Westminster and St James's, London, in March 1978, Scotland Yard could hardly be blamed for deciding that a new professional gang had moved into the area. Between March 1978 and January 1979 he committed sixty-six burglaries.

He was not in the business for big-time rewards. He simply went into it for spending-money – his targets were the petty-cash boxes in offices, the tea and coffee money left by secretaries in desk-drawers. During the ten months his total haul was £2650.

Because of his activities, police set up a special squad of detectives. They were convinced there was more behind the burglaries in the VIP office area than met the eye. But they failed to trap him. He was only caught through his own inefficiency – he plunged through a skylight in an office in St James's Place, Westminster, and broke a leg. There was nothing he could do but wait until help – and the law – arrived.

His confession staggered the Yard. He told them: 'I entered offices in the St James's and Victoria areas of London by breaking ground-floor windows and escaping through skylights or fire-escapes. I always chose streets where I could get from one office to another across the rooftops. On average I did three or four a night.' But, as Arthur himself was to admit, what at the start had been exciting was becoming boring routine. He began comparing it with a dull daytime legitimate job. 'It became so regular it was no longer exciting.'

For Arthur, burglary was a compulsion. He had nineteen previous convictions. As Arthur began a five-year sentence in 1979 a Scotland Yard detective said: 'It did not seem possible for one man to do so much. His confession cleared up pages of unsolved incidents in the area crime-book.' Perhaps the judge summed it up best. 'It would be difficult to imagine a sadder case.' Well, maybe. But at least Arthur is alive. Being a cat burglar is a perilous business.

A year earlier, in 1978, there had been a tragic end for a twenty-five-year-old man who, with another man, had decided to earn a comfortable living by burglarising homes in the high-rise blocks in London's East End. He had to limit his takings to cash and jewellery (it is hard to be a cat burglar and flee with the colour television). The method was simple but hair-raising. The high-rise cat burglar simply took the lift to the top floor and walked on to the roof. Then he lowered himself by a rope on to the ledges which jutted out between the floors. Clinging like a fly on to the brickwork, he inched his way to the nearest window to gain entry, but the wind – always an occupational hazard – proved his undoing. The body of the twenty-five-year-old burglar was found at the foot of a twenty-five-storey tower-block in Poplar. He had died from multiple injuries consistent with falling from the upper levels. Police said they were sure he had been trying to break into a flat when he fell.

Why become a cat burglar? The excitement, the easy pickings – the usual attractions. For twenty-eight-year-old Steven, however, there was a very compelling reason. He had no legs. But his disability was compensated for by arms of enormous strength. His was another sad case. He had left home as a teenager and contracted frostbite in his legs through sleeping rough. When frostbite turned to gangrene, Steven – then aged sixteen – had to have both legs amputated.

Ten years later he launched himself as a cat burglar – and created his own crime-wave in southern England. He hauled himself up drainpipes of homes. He even scaled Brighton pier's thirty-foot girders to rob the bar. But his downfall (or the end of his burglary career) came after forty-one burglaries. He broke into a cruising club and set off a secret burglar-alarm. When police-car crews surrounded the building they were astonished to find a cat burglar without legs.

If ever there was a case when the leniency of the courts actively helped and encouraged a burglar to go to the top of the criminal league, it was that of thirty-three-year-old David, King of the Cat Burglars.

For seventeen years magistrates and judges bent over backwards to try to keep David out of jail. During that time he ran up twenty-two convictions for theft, burglary and suspicion of being on enclosed premises. The highest sentence of three years came towards the end of his career and before he made his real money. His criminal record is littered with courts placing David on probation, becoming harsher with fines, followed by prison-sentences for brief periods, only to be suspended again by the courts. This meant that as long as he was not caught during the period of suspension he did not have to go behind bars.

It took twenty-two previous convictions and a final spate of cat burglaries, which netted David at least £500,000, for the courts to exhaust their leniency. In 1979 at the Old Bailey, Recorder Miss Jean Southworth, QC, sentenced David to ten years after telling him that he had 'abused the charity of the courts for far too long'.

I watched David in court and as he returned to his cell to begin his sentence and, though he was not smiling exactly, he was smug on two counts: first, that on his own admission he had the proceeds of his final spree of £500,000 in a secret safe-deposit box, the police not having a clue to its location; and, secondly, that with good behaviour he could be paroled any time after serving only one-third of the ten years.

David was a professional. His brisk walk from the Old Bailey dock to the cells revealed his superb fitness. At five feet four inches tall and weighing ten stone, strength flowed throughout his entire body. Police have no doubt that he will keep fit while in jail. To 'earn' the £500,000 nest egg in his final crime fling, David trained every day. As he told the Yard on his arrest, his training consisted of running, weight-lifting, climbing and, he added with a smile, 'jumping'.

It was his ability to jump, swing and climb that enabled him to gain access where most victims feel secure – unguarded windows high in hotel blocks and flats all over London. As Detective Inspector Jeffrey Rees, the officer who eventually arrested him, said succinctly: 'Nobody expected a burglar to come in through the air.'

These 'missions impossible' won David the Yard title 'best cat burglar of all time'. A typical example of his daring was his raid on the VIP hotel, Claridges. It would be hard to find a hotel in the capital which has better security. Heads of state and diplomats from all over the world stop there. To ensure peace of mind from assassins, kidnappers and thieves, the hotel has its own security force, including several ex-Yard men.

High on their list of priorities is a close watch on loiterers or visitors who appear uncertain. David knew this. He strode through the front door with no hesitancy, no stopping to ask porters for directions. Straight to the lift and seventh floor. From his observations outside, he had spotted scaffolding protruding from the sheer face of the hotel wall. On the seventh floor – and a short jump away from the base of the scaffolding – was the open window of a hotel room. If he missed the jump, it would mean certain death. There was nothing for seven floors to break his fall and only concrete at the bottom.

On the seventh floor David slipped out of a window in the

corridor, climbed on to the scaffolding, and leaped Tarzan-fashion through the window of a room rented by Mrs Della Koenig. David's stealing policy was never to take anything which could not be slipped into his pockets, being limited thereby to jewellery and cash.

Minutes later David walked out with jewels worth a minimum conservative estimate of £46,000. He easily let himself out of the hotel room – the locks are designed to prevent people getting in, not out. The lift to the main foyer. This time he confidently walked up to a porter and instructed the man in the Claridges uniform to call him a taxi. He gave a modest tip (he was later to say that large tippers are remembered by staff).

He had a ready answer if, on breaking through a window, he should discover the premises occupied. He would pretend he was a plumber on a repair job. He was provided with a chance to demonstrate his skill with the ready answer during a break-in at the Mayfair home of Lady Philippa MacAlpine. He had just pocketed jewels worth £25,000 when, walking into the lounge, he found himself face to face with Lady Philippa. 'It's all right, lady, I've seen the guv'nor. I've just finished the repair.' Leaving a rather puzzled Lady Philippa wondering what the repair was, David walked confidently out of the front door. The burglary was not discovered until later.

Exactly how much, and from whom, David gained on his last spree is not known. On his own admission to detectives he put the figure at £500,000. He was caught only because detectives, faced with an epidemic of cat burglaries in the West End, asked their computer at the Yard for the man with this method most likely to be responsible. One name only came up: David's.

The Yard initially set out to catch him red-handed. The secret Criminal Intelligence Department was assigned to 'shadow' him, but within hours of the start of the operation David spotted his tail along a London street. Concluding he was under observation, he immediately slipped into a betting-shop, hoping there would be a rear exit. Instead, it became his trap. Rather than lose him, the police moved in to arrest him. As Detective Inspector Rees told me: 'Spotting his "shadow" was some achievement. It is something far better criminals than he have failed to notice.'

On his arrest, David used his final skill. From previous court appearances he had gained considerable expertise in legal machinations and the system. He knew what to say, what not to say, what to admit to when faced with damning evidence (such as fingerprints), and what he could say to detectives in the certainty it could not be used in evidence against him.

He knew now that if he confessed to all the crimes the police were questioning him about he could face a long sentence. Cheekily he told the detectives: 'I'm staring ten years in the face if I admit to all those burglaries.' He admitted two burglaries – that at Claridges and a second at Lady Philippa's. Evidence in both cases was overwhelming.

The police also suspected him of burglarising other flats, including two in Grosvenor Square, in which jewellery valued at over £115,000 was taken. He pleaded not guilty to these charges. His defence was that he was not the only cat burglar in London with the *modus operandi* that fitted. Therefore, he did not want every job in London 'thrown at him'. After telling a jury there were many other cat burglars, he was found not guilty of burglarising one home in Grosvenor Square and the jury was discharged from giving a verdict on two other burglaries.

He hoped his ploy had succeeded when he faced the judge, Recorder Miss Jean Southworth, for sentencing, but his face darkened when she told him: 'Your skills don't stop at being apparently the only cat burglar in this category required to commit the two offences in this case – certainly the one at Claridges, which involved climbing and jumping through a window at height, and you are the only one who came up on the criminal record computer.

'You also have skills which go to the conduct of your defence. Over the years you have had criminal experience and considerable experience of the courts and juries and, now that I know two counts are not to be proceeded with, I can see this.'

Being sentenced to ten years was bad enough. But there was an additional punishment. The judge made a criminal bankruptcy order for £71,000. The importance of this was that the judge appreciated that none of David's stolen fortune had been recovered by the police. He had admitted to detectives that he kept his jewels in a safe-deposit box – 'somewhere in London' – and that he kept a hidden key. A second key was held by his mate – a man not yet identified by the police. Both keys are required to open his Aladdin's Cave.

On paper David had no visible assets. He lived with his mother in a council flat in east London. He did not even own a car. So nothing can be seized. However, the bankruptcy order remains in force until the £71,000 is recovered. This means that when David is released from prison (he can expect to serve four or five years) police will be waiting and watching. Any time he obtains any goods, they can be seized. David knows this. In reality, it is unlikely that the money will be recovered by the authorities, but it does ensure that David will not lead too comfortable a life when he is freed. He will still have to keep looking over his shoulder wherever he goes. Apart from the police, he is fully aware that the hard villains of the underworld also know he has a fortune – and they would like to relieve him of it. The chances are that if he survives prison without injury he is likely to be abducted on release and encouraged by torture to reveal the location of his jewel hoard and the secret of entry.

The Drug Burglars

A person turns to burglary for one or a variety of reasons. Apart from the obvious ones, a recent motive is a need for and dependence on drugs.

In the sixties chemists' shops were likely targets. Security was lax, and pusher and customer alike found that a simple break-in saved them the trouble of tricking doctors into writing prescriptions. As burglaries at chemists' shops increased, so did the concern of the police and the pharmaceutical profession. Safes, strongboxes and other devices to secure pills and addictive drugs soon discouraged this trend.

More recently the problem of addicts' supplies has been solved in another way. Addicts commit burglary, the profits from which can buy the next fix. The son and daughter of a well-known London politician resorted to this when their heroin supply dried up. They were sad cases and easily caught. A neighbour spotted the politician's son 'gabbling and shaking'. His sister arrived, and both of them ran away. The police were called, and the son told detectives: 'I need money for a fix. I am on heroin and need some quickly.' Then he admitted burglary at the neighbour's flat. He had broken in and stolen jewellery worth £2000. His sister had not entered the flat, but had acted as lookout.

What disturbed the police about this case was the ease with which the son had sold the jewels – and the price obtained. The boy gave details of his trip to a Bond Street jeweller's. The staff there had examined the stolen jewels and offered the boy £300 in cash. The police were able to recover the jewels.

This couple were fortunate. Because of their arrest, their burglary activities were halted at the start. They had been put in touch with drug experts and had taken the advice to move away from London and the drug scene.

The Chimney Burglars

Probably the most extraordinary method of burglary is the chimney break-in. Many modern homes, equipped with gas or oil central heating, do not have a chimney. Those that do usually have chimneys not large enough for a small man. However, across the nation there are many older-type houses that have giant chimneys – often a complex system running through the interior of a house. In Victorian days these chimneys were cleaned by boys who literally climbed with brushes through the network.

The boys are gone – but the chimneys remain a very popular attraction to burglars. Seldom is a chimney rigged with a burglar-alarm, and entry by this method does not involve any forcing or breaking. Police are convinced that many a successful burglar has risked life and limb to gain entrance by this method.

The most bizarre evidence to show that this method is still in use was obtained in 1976 by police at Bradford in West Yorkshire. It also solved the mystery of the disappearance of a well-known burglar named James Scott-Hall. He vanished in 1970 and police, asked to make enquires by relatives, could find no leads – until 1976, when workmen, called into an office complex to solve problems with the heating system, found a decomposed body in the chimney. It was identified as Scott-Hall's from a set of dentures made while he was in Lancaster Prison in 1967.

In a reconstruction of events by police, all the evidence pointed to Scott-Hall having climbed to the top of the chimney above offices in Eldon Place, Bradford. Being a thin man, he squeezed himself into the chimney for a descent into the offices inside the building. The chimney entrance was only fourteen inches square. This would not have been a problem for Scott-Hall. Inside the building the chimney complex widened. What terrible events followed no one will ever know. Scott-Hall may have slipped; he certainly ended up at the bottom of one chimney which once had a fireplace that had since been bricked up. If he was conscious, his screams for help when he found he could not get back up and out were never heard. He died inside the black hole of the chimney – and he remained there for six years until workmen discovered his body.

The Church Burglars

The Saxon church nestling in the little village in Middlesex, not far from the quieter parts of the River Thames, had been well inspected by a team weeks before the burglary. Apart from the obviously easily saleable items in the church, the lookouts had made one vital discovery. One had followed the churchwarden into the church just before closing-time and noted that the key used for locking up was kept in a drawer.

When the key was found to be missing one evening several weeks later, this caused mild surprise. That it might have been taken by burglars did not occur to the warden.

The village church had been built in Saxon times. It had survived the wars and was a focal point of community life. Because it was a place of worship the doors were always open during the daytime. Worshippers and the merely curious were welcomed by the Vicar or his churchwardens. The church did close down at night. The Vicar reluctantly accepted that the huge ancient wood doors had to be closed and the large iron key turned in the lock – a precaution to keep out chance vandals.

The church was steeped in history. There was valuable plate on the walls, pictures worth thousands of pounds, and Jacobean chairs that would grace a London antique dealer's showrooms.

Security of church buildings can in no way be said to have moved with the lawless times of the outside world. Each morning when the key turned in the lock on the church doors to call in the daily visitors, the Vicar or his warden would place it for safe keeping in a drawer in a table in the vestry. The drawer was not locked. This type of security cover is well known to those burglars who specialise in helping themselves from God's places of worship. There is little risk, for the burglars can mingle and tour churches viewed as possible targets, posing as sightseers or even worshippers. But their eyes are not looking to God. Their concern is the valuables – and how easy or difficult their removal.

The burglars did not take the key in order to open up during the night. They had taken it in the hope that the doors would not be locked – as proved to be the case.

It is not known what time the gang arrived. It was between late evening and dawn. When the warden arrived the next day he sensed the nakedness of the church. Every item of plate had been removed, as had the pictures and, of course, the Jacobean chairs. For the burglars it was not a huge haul – about £14,000 cash in it for them. They had buyers fixed up days before the raid, and it is likely that the stolen items had already been delivered to the first receiver before the Vicar was asleep the night after the raid.

The police guess is that within forty-eight hours the proceeds from the looted church had changed hands as much as four times before being crated at a dockside warehouse for 'export'. It is no secret that, of all antiques, items from British churches have a special value to foreign collectors. Not, of course, that anyone would acknowledge that the antiques delivered to the Washington house or to the Rome mansion had been taken from a church. But experts in the trade say that buyers can sense the likely background of such items when they are first advised of their availability.

The Cheap-Day Burglars

We come to the cheap-day burglar, the city dweller who exploits the railways 'cheap day return'. He joins the passengers for a day in the country. He rarely operates on a rainy day. No one likes getting wet, and a burglar walking in the rain attracts more attention even if he poses as an insurance salesman or a visiting relative. He does not wish to take a taxi to or from the railway station, because he knows that investigating detectives check with taxi drivers, who often have very good memories.

In the stockbroker belt of Surrey, for example, the burglar who arrives by train on a day excursion is blamed for many of the thirty or so burglaries that are logged each day. According to Surrey Police Chief Constable Peter Matthews, the burglar of the eighties is strictly a twentieth-century product. Forget the flat cap and striped jersey. 'He commutes just like his victims but in reverse,' says Mr Matthews.

On arrival at his target destination the burglar will walk around the housing area closest to the station – those houses often being the most expensive because they are so handy for the trains. He is even likely to have a ploughman's lunch at the local pub before striking. Often he will force a rear window or find an unlocked door. He is likely to borrow a carrier bag from the kitchen cupboard. After selecting items easily carried away, he will hurry back to the station and be home in time to miss the evening rush hour.

Murder

The pleasant detached house in Whitehall Road, Woodford, Essex, appeared an ideal target for the three-strong burglary gang. It faced forest land across a fairly busy road. It was well maintained, and the contents could be expected to produce a worthwhile haul. There was a short drive to the front door. They had already tried other houses in the area without success. Their method of operating was standard. Two positioned themselves as lookouts close by in case a police patrol car was in the area. The third walked up to the house and peered through the first window. If it seemed empty, he would ring the doorbell. If someone answered, the excuse would be a wrong address, then a quick apology and departure.

Burglary had been good for the trio. The nearby forest at Epping had provided an ideal 'storehouse'. After a raid the spoils were wrapped in plastic and buried in a prepared hole, eliminating the risk of taking goods home to friends. The trio felt the chances of being caught were minimal. They were fortunate enough to link up with a big-time gang of receivers, and business was booming.

Recent snow covered the pavement and forest. There were only a few hours of daylight left. A quick thumbs-up sign after the first appraisal by the lookouts, and the burglar broke in. It was the beginning of a raid that was to turn into a total nightmare for the three young white boys, and, for one, it was to end in horrible terror and physical violence.

Eighty-two hours earlier, two schoolgirls returning home to that very house had discovered a horrific murder. Twenty-nine-year-old Linda Farrow, a beautiful former inspector of croupiers at the International Sporting Club in London, had driven her car up to the driveway and started to unload her shopping. Six months earlier she had left her husband, who was nearly blind, to live with her lover. He worked at a local market. They had rented the house as a love nest until divorces had been finalised.

On 18 January, inside the hallway of the house, she had been horribly murdered. A freezer-knife had been used on her neck as her attacker had held her by the hair, face downwards on the floor of the hall. With sawing motions he had virtually cut her head off before fleeing.

After the discovery of the murder, there had been frenzied police activity at the house all that day and the next. The scientists had departed with their clues. The police vehicles were back at the local station – all except one. A CID car with two officers had been sent to continue the interview with Linda's lover. The trio had walked back to the house from the market. Unknown to the burglars, they were inside the house when the burglars went into action. The burglar walked up the drive and pressed his nose against the window of the lounge. Just then the Murder Squad detectives inside spotted him.

As all officers are well aware, it is not unusual for a killer to revisit the scene of a crime. After exchanging glances, the reaction a split second later was electrifying. The burglar, still unaware that he had chosen a murder house, assumed it was occupied and took to his heels. As he rushed from the drive, his two lookouts also took off – one making a huge leap over a fence into an adjoining garden. Unlike many residents who spot burglars at a window, there was no hesitation by the two Murder Squad officers. They reacted even faster. Leaving an astonished lover standing in the lounge, they went in pursuit.

Reaction from a householder may be unusual, but the fleeing burglar who had pressed his nose against the window had no idea that his pursuers were police officers. When they Rugby-tackled him, the burglar put up a ferocious fight – all boots and fists.

Minutes later he was being hauled back inside the house. Because he was still fighting furiously, the officers holding him with armlocks forced him to the floor in the hallway – on top of the still heavily bloodstained carpet. A big police hunt was launched immediately by the Murder Squad for the fleeing two. A police dog soon found one in the forest.

Both men were viewed by the detectives as key suspects for murder. At first they could hardly take in what was happening to them. Desperate not to be involved in murder, and with the fear of a long prison-sentence staring them in the face, they began blurting out their confession. 'We're only burglars,' they screamed in terror.

Maybe they were lucky being caught. Worse was in store for the third. He had fled not knowing what had happened to his mates. He had no idea they had picked a house where the blood was hardly dry. He returned to his home, celebrating his escape. Then a few drinks at the local, acting the big confident lad. At least, that was how it was until later that night, when the heavy mob from the local crime syndicate arrived.

The gangsters broke the news to him smiling. His two mates had been arrested. The cops were swarming around. Funny, wasn't it, that he was the only one of the trio not caught? Strange, wasn't it, that the cops had not been to his home? Even more amusing, here he was enjoying a game of snooker and a pint, happy as a sandboy, while his two mates were inside for a job that they had all been involved in.

His protests that he honestly did not know what they were talking about cut no ice. The strong-armed men with their cold grins told him what had happened – he had obviously 'grassed' (informed) on his mates to save himself. There were too many at that game nowadays, he was told. A few examples had to be set.

He was 'invited' to walk outside. It was, as the saying goes, an offer he could not refuse. His feet were not on the ground anyway. The heavies, in their smart suits and still smiling, sandwiched him between their bodies and walked him. Outside, the long razor flashed in the cold night air – a terrible slash on his throat. It was not a killing slash. Just to leave a scar for life. The heavies were very pleasant about it. He was being let off lightly – just a warning of what happens to people stupid enough to talk to the police. They had their own skins to think about. Business was booming and no one wanted any hitches, did they?

After the terror punishment, the burglar crept home to bandage his throat. The blood had soaked his shirt and suit.

It was in this condition that the Murder Squad found him. He had even more of a job satisfying them that he had not been the killer – that the blood was his and not Linda's.

60

A terrifying story – but burglary can turn into murder. Basically, burglars do not want violence, but more and more are turning to violence to escape capture.

Only the exceptional cases receive prominence in the media. The growth of violence in burglary has itself diminished the impact on the public and the interest of the press. One exception during 1979 was the trial of a gang of burglars who murdered Carl Bridgewater, a newspaper-boy who stumbled on the raiders by accident while on his delivery-round. The burglars were not masked, and to silence Carl so that he could not identify them to the police he was shot dead at point-blank range with a shotgun. Only one of the gang, fifty-one-year-old Patrick Molloy, escaped lightly with a twelve-year sentence for manslaughter. Molloy, of no fixed address, who confessed that he had previously committed 200 burglaries, was the only one who admitted he had been ransacking Yew Tree Farm at Wordsley, West Midlands. He admitted he was upstairs when Carl was murdered in a ground-floor room, and his admission helped the police. Two others – James Robinson, forty-five, and Vincent Hickey, twenty-five, were jailed for life with recommendations from the judge, Mr Justice Drake, that each should serve at least twenty-five years. Michael Hickey, only seventeen, also convicted of murder, was ordered to be detained during Her Majesty's pleasure. The judge described Robinson and Vincent Hickey as 'evil and greedy men'.

In 1978 there were 158 cases in the Metropolitan Police area in which the victim of a burglary was subjected to major violence. These figures are not included in the burglary statistics because they come under the more serious classification 'crimes of violence'. But burglary cases have included the knifing to death of a woman, murder, rape and attempting to destroy the crime by arson.

Rape

The gloved right hand of the burglar gropes along the wall, trying to locate the light-switch in the dark of a room safely sealed from the outside world by heavy-lined curtains across a double window. Ray is permitting himself a slight security gamble. But it is worth it for the luxury of being able to see. He is convinced the flat he is raiding is empty.

At the age of thirty-two he is making a good living from burglary. His start in the burglary business had been modest. Initially, after leaving secondary school, his jobs had been legitimate. He had worked as a shop sales assistant and then tried his hand as a double-glazing salesman. But he was lacking in experience and maturity, and was sacked. Then he switched to working as a 'knocker', joining a team of men who toured selected areas and called at homes telling the occupants their antiques could be sold on the spot for cash. The initial knock at the door often resulted in an invitation to examine articles. His colleagues soon informed Ray that 'extra' could be made on the side – by selling tips to burglars. There was no risk to Ray and his 'knocker' friends. After identifying homes suitable for a raid they ensured they were miles away with watertight alibis when the burglary took place. He quickly discovered that there was a huge market for stolen goods. Buyers in Sweden and the States wanted antique guns, in particular. The Portuguese collectors sought stolen British porcelain. Paintings could be shipped to South America within hours of a burglary. Tipping the syndicate was fine, but Ray wanted the big money provided by burglary. He decided to go all the way. He had been on more than 150 successful raids. Each time he was in action he lived on his nerves. Now he felt the adrenalin racing as his hand found the light-switch. It was pumping through his bloodstream from the second he started to force the front door. A slight pressure on the switch and a second later the room is flooded with light. He waits a few seconds to take in the scene. He is in a bedroom. There is someone asleep in the double bed. It is a woman – alone.

Whether she is pretty or not is no matter. She immediately becomes a threat to his safety. His reflex action is to race to the bed as the woman stirs. His first action in fact is to rip out the bedside telephone. The woman's eyes, still full of sleep, are open now. She has not time really to take in the situation or scream when Ray throws himself on her. The woman is terrified. She freezes with fear and offers no resistance. Ray rapes her. He later flees, taking nothing. The burglary in the south London flat is just one of a small but rapidly growing number of burglaries which in 1979 ended in either murder, or rape, or other violence.

But what suddenly, in a matter of moments, turns burglars into killers? What triggers off rape? For basically burglary is a non-violent crime. The leniency of the courts to burglars who do not use violence actively discourages rape and violence.

According to policemen and psychologists with whom I have talked, all burglars are potential users of violence when at work. The excitement caused by the thought-processes when a burglar goes into action pumps adrenalin into the bloodstream. The motives of the burglars are greed and lust, for money and for possessions. Once in action the burglar has created for himself an emotional state of highly charged lust; but the inital lust for possessions and for property is so knife-edged that it can be instantly switched to lust for sex on discovering an unprotected woman, or lust for self-

62

preservation in the case of Carl Bridgewater. With huge amounts of adrenalin already in circulation, one can understand why burglaries turn to violence.

Examine the facts. First, study must be made of burglars who, like those in the Carl Bridgewater case, went armed to a burglary. This is classified as 'aggravated burglary' – those offences classified by the police in which the offender is known to have had with him a firearm, weapon of offence (such as a cosh) or explosives.

In England and Wales in 1971 there were 243 'aggravated burglaries' in homes. In 1978 there were 528 – over a hundred per cent more. Of course, the figure only relates to burglaries in which the police discovered such weapons were carried. This means the burglars either fled leaving the evidence, or were arrested, or left victims alive to tell the tale. Countless more burglaries were undoubtedly 'aggravated' but, because there is no positive evidence, cannot be classified as such. The hundred per cent increase is likely to be a very conservative estimate.

How many burglaries have turned to rape? All the indications are that during the late seventies there was a steady increase. The police do not centrally collate statistics of crimes that start off as burglary and end as rape. The only guide is the total volume of rape in England and Wales. In 1971 there were 784 rapes. By 1978 the figure had risen to 1243. The police are confident that among the 1243 there are several hundred rapes by burglars who by unexpected circumstances were triggered into becoming sex fiends.

The Ingenuity of the Burglar

The ingenuity of the burglar determined to take other people's property is limitless. The latest dodges are the intriguing developments of basic break-in methods. These are known to the police, but few householders are aware of the refinements.

A good example is the hurled-brick method. Robert, who lives in Dulwich, south London, was a recent victim. A successful executive, he lives in a modernised older-style house on the outskirts of the area well known for its modern and expensive properties. Because of the age of the house, there is only a small front garden separating it from the footpath and main highway.

It was four o'clock on a bitterly cold February morning when a half-brick, hurled from the pavement area, shattered the glass of the ground-floor lounge-window and thudded on the fitted carpets inside the house. The fastest response came from Robert's eleven-year-old daughter. She screamed at the sudden noise that shattered the stillness of the morning and ran from her bedroom on the first floor, directly over the lounge, into her parents' adjoining room. Robert leaped out of bed. He was shaking sleep from his head with every quick step. He had given no thought to how he might tackle an intruder when he burst into the lounge after running down the stairs.

His dash down the stairs had been instinctive gut reaction. He threw on the light-switch – and discovered an empty room. There was only the half-brick and jagged glass that had been contained by the curtains. He was more aware of the icy wind blowing in from across the snow outside and through the shattered window than of anything else. The central heating had been kept on all night, maintaining the house temperature at 70 degrees, and the whole family, even in the height of winter, still wore lightweight pyjamas.

'We immediately decided it was the senseless work of hooligans,' Robert told me. 'The street outside was deserted. I immediately tucked the curtains up tight against the broken glass to keep out as much of the cold as I could. I looked outside again, but there was not a soul about. Then I called the police.'

The police were already in the area. In a short, sharp period of ten minutes half a dozen houses in the area had suffered the same fate. There had been no break-in at all. The possibility that it was the work of a drunken party reveller returning home was among the theories considered by the police.

The local builder did brisk trade as Robert and the other victims pleaded for the fastest possible service to replace the broken glass panes. Dulwich returned to normality. The local home-beat police officer made a point of carrying out a special 4.00 a.m. patrol for the next few days.

On the eighth day the matter was explained. Not a noise had been heard in the night. However, three of the six householders opened their lounge-doors in the morning to find the room icy cold. There was no broken glass this time. Simply there was no glass in the window. Burglars had been back. The new glass had been sealed in place with putty. Window-frame putty takes days, if not weeks, to set like concrete. The gang had simply walked up to the windows, run a sharp knife around the setting putty, and removed it. Then they had simply taken out the new panes of glass. The operation was done in total silence.

'They put my pane of glass down on the ground beneath the window,' said Robert. 'At least it wasn't broken. It was a simple matter to put it back and get fresh putty to seal it back in place. They had come in through the glassless window and only taken items in the lounge. The biggest was my music centre. It was not that new. It was worth about £1500, and I had plans to replace it with an even better set of equipment. They also took my television and rented video. My loss was about £3000. Funny thing was that I was not too upset by the event. I was fully insured. I had an index-linked policy which guaranteed replacing new for old. I was paid out very quickly and was able to go out and buy the new equipment I had wanted without any problem or trying to trade in the old gear. I was not out of pocket at all, because the broken window was covered by insurance as well.'

It was a similar story at the three other homes in the area. Only the immediate room in which the window-pane was removed was burglarised. The hauls were very similar – colour televisions, hi fi and other electronic equipment, plus any obviously expensive furnishings, such as silver candlesticks.

The Dulwich incident is by no means an isolated one. The brick-through-the-window method has cropped up in many other areas. Police are now fully aware of this method of operation – but that does not mean that it has been abandoned by the burglary business.

4 The Receivers

The man hunched low over his snooker cue in the all-day drinking club in west London was about to pot the black ball in a winning shot when the telephone a few yards from the table rang. In an instant all concentration on the game was gone. He had been playing at the table all through the long afternoon. Many times he had looked in anticipation at the telephone on the wall. When other members had used it to make calls he had become restless – impatient for the conversations to end so that the phone would not register 'engaged' if the call he was waiting for came. He was awaiting 'orders' from the managing director of a wholesale company with offices in a plush tower-block in the City of London. Now, at last, the phone was ringing, and the snooker cue was placed hurriedly in its rest. The player took the few strides to the receiver.

'Steve?' asked the man in the City. 'You free?'

The voice of the caller was surprisingly coarse and harsh. It had always betrayed a background of south-east London slums, and now that a cash fortune in the bank had bought affluence and business-power the man no longer tried to disguise his accent.

The snooker-player kept his answer brief. 'Yep,' he replied. The voice of the caller was so familiar that he did not even have to acknowledge the businessman as Ken. There had been many hundreds of such calls to the same club over the years. Steve had never trusted telephones – there was always the chance of a crossed line or, worse still, the police tapping it. But the phone was his lifeline, and he had accepted the risks, minimising danger by always keeping conversations as brief as possible.

'I can place some silver. It's got to be by next week,' said the caller.

Steve's reply was to the point. 'OK, I'll be in touch.'

That was all there was to it. The snooker player returned to the table, potted black and, together with his opponent, returned to the bar and ordered beers. Business had just been transacted.

It was in fact an order for a silver burglary. The telephone caller had been a professional receiver of stolen goods. The snooker players were two operatives in his network. They were among his contacts who specialised in silver thefts. They could clear a house of silver in a quarter of an hour. Napkin-rings, ashtrays, rose-bowls, jugs, candlesticks, hand-mirrors, brooches, coffee-pots and trays were their speciality. They were the workers. For every £1000 worth of goods they were paid only £100. The receiver's explanation of the apparently low price had been given long ago. Many of the stolen items had to be melted down. The workmanship that had gone into the making of the items counted for nothing; the value, he claimed, was purely in the metal. It was easy to sell and cut out the risk of stolen items being identified. For Steve and his mate it was cash in hand and no tax. They had long ago accepted that it was the receiver – the middle-man for burglars – who made the big money from the crime. Ken, the businessman who called the snooker players, was a classic example. His £150,000 mansion in Surrey, his chauffeur, his latest-model Jaguar car, and his personal bank-balance had all been provided by burglary.

Without the likes of Ken the burglary business would be less efficient. There is little point in stealing if the 'hot' goods cannot be quickly and easily sold. The police estimate that for every dozen burglars there is a man like Ken – the 'Mr Fixits' of the burglary business, the men who market the stolen goods, the men who give the orders to the burglars, the men who pay the burglars only ten per cent of real value because they know they have the whip-hand. They are ready to accept the proceeds from their burglars within hours of the raid being completed. The burglars are in turn paid cash at the hand-over and are then free from incriminating evidence by the time the police hunt begins.

Ken is a typical example of a successful receiver. He owns an import–export company. On paper it is totally respectable. It is registered at Company House, and Ken is listed as managing director and chief shareholder. His wife is shown as the company secretary. The annual business-returns are always made promptly. His key employees are all hand-selected. They know Ken's real business and are as deeply involved in the recycling of stolen goods as he is. But on the face of it they are all hard-working respectable businessmen, wheeling and dealing mainly in costume jewellery. An inspection of their invoices would reveal only that the accounts were meticulously kept. The VAT inspectors have never had a query. But the legitimate part of the business is simply a cover for the illicit money-making transactions involving the proceeds of burglary. The local police have never suspected, for a key rule of the firm is that all the burglaries that Ken commissions are carried out in areas well away from London, and the burglars are never permitted to visit the company premises – a further step to avoid any chance of the police becoming suspicious.

The three-hour business-lunch in the packed Manchester club had been a relaxed affair and the conversation affable. The luncheon host, owner of a small chain of High Street supermarkets, puffed at his cigar, sipped his vintage port, and said to his guest very casually, 'By the way, I could use some chocolates.'

It was not a suggestion that the waiter should be summoned to produce After Eight mints. The guest, owner of a Blackpool club, knew exactly what was meant. He replied with confidence: 'I'll see what can be done.' No further mention was made of the chocolates, and the lunch ended with handshakes as their chauffeur-driven cars arrived. 'I'll be in touch,' the guest said by way of a parting.

The reality of the situation – which is repeated daily across the nation – was that a chain of events had been initiated that resulted in three men breaking into a confectionery warehouse in the early hours of the morning three weeks later. None of the burglars knew of the existence of the men who had enjoyed that fine business-lunch. They had simply received a 'commission' passed down through the chain of command that governs the sub-culture of the burglary world.

Five days after the break-in at the warehouse, chocolates with a retail value of £6000 had changed hands four times. Then the chocolates were delivered, with full invoices, to the chain of stores whose owner had said, 'I could use some chocolates.' They became the week's 'star attraction – buy of the week', eagerly promoted by managers suitably impressed by the attractive deal achieved by their boss in the purchase of the special consignment.

No member of staff had a clue that he was in fact handling stolen goods. Only a protracted probe by Fraud Squad experts into the chain-store accounts and invoicing system would have produced a clue that they had not been purchased at such an attractive price simply by shrewd buying. But there was no chance of any such action. There had never been a hint of any impropriety about the successful businessman who had built up his chain stores. He had become accepted in his community as a pillar of respectable society.

Burglary has its own very specialised command-structure. It is comparable with the organisation of a major multi-national business organisation with a far-ranging network of subsidiary companies with widely diversified interests. At 'boardroom' level are the businessmen such as the owner of the chain stores who gets progressively richer from a largely legitimate business-base topped up with 'cream' from the burglary business. These men are so far removed from the actual event that they have little or no fear of ever having an accusing finger pointed at them – let alone facing suspicion of criminal conspiracy to commit burglary.

The driving factor that constantly stimulates the whole organisation is that the overwhelming majority of major burglaries are carried out strictly to fulfil an order. Because of the demand the burglary business flourishes. The whole structure of the successful burglary-business network leans heavily on, and very much revolves around, receivers. Receivers are the managers of the burglary industry – the senior executives who act according to the whims and fancies and demands of the 'directors', the major purchasers of the goods. Receivers commission the crimes from a network of operatives. Often the orders first go to 'deputy managers', the men in the know when it comes to placing the contracts with the suitable specialist.

Very much like the placing of genuine contracts for work projects, burglary projects that cannot be fulfilled by the first operative approached can usually be placed with a recommended colleague. Often the operative will accept the order, and then sub-contract to another burglar who is more available. Each time the order is passed down the line a commission is sought. This is the highly professional network of the men at the hub of the huge burglary industry.

Amateurs have no place in the network in which goods are 'ordered'. For the professional receiver, the amateur burglar is a real danger. The amateur is most likely to be caught, and contribute to the lowly police statistics of those crimes classified as 'cleared up'. But it's not the danger of the amateurs being caught that makes the receivers dissociate themselves from them; it's the risk that the amateurs could bring about the downfall of the receiver and in turn the collapse of a whole company. Amateur burglars account for as much as seventy per cent of recorded offences, but they are mainly youngsters and opportunists. They comprise the majority of those burglars who are actually caught by police. It is the professional burglars, who are 'hired' by a network of receivers, who carry out thefts to order – and seldom get caught.

The graduation from amateur to professional burglar usually takes place in prison. Experienced criminals in prison – usually convicted for serious crimes other than burglary – effect introduction and recruitment to professional crime syndicates. The amateur burglar only goes to prison after repeated crimes. Professionals view these as ideal material for moulding into a professional. Once within the organisation of a professional gang the new recruit is accepted by the receiver.

The police are convinced that there are many thousands of such firms whose untaxed fortunes come from the proceeds of crime.

They range from firms dealing as wholesalers in food and wine to pawnshops and scrap-metal dealers. A very large part of the vast volume of goods stolen in Britain is today recycled into legitimate business outlets, such as the High Street shops, through middle-men and wholesale organisations specially set up by receivers of stolen goods.

The bottom would drop out of the burglary business overnight if the thieves could not find ready buyers. The reality of the situation is that there is a huge army of businessmen who do very nicely indeed out of burglary with little personal risk. The huge profit they are able to make from the burglary business, without ever having to enter a house or other type of premises themselves, results in actively encouraging crime on the one hand, while maintaining a personal respectable front on the other.

These men are the buyers of goods stolen in burglary. They are the middle-men, who have created a vast recycling industry for stolen goods. They come in all forms – from the Mayfair jeweller who as good as admits that he knows that the diamond engagement-ring he is being offered has been stolen, when he calmly looks the seller in the eye and offers a hundredth of the price in cash, which is eagerly accepted, to the market street-trader with the fast turnover of goods.

In this chapter a close look is taken at their activities – and their relationships with the police. The example chosen details how complex the disposal of items from burglary can become. It involves a case in which I witnessed this first-hand, because a burglar who became greedy hatched a plot in which he decided to use me as the unwitting middle-man. It revealed a world of deals, double-crosses and betrayals, which would have done justice to power-games played by businessmen set on making a personal fortune at anyone's expense.

The saga began simply enough. During a weekend, when the offices in the City of London had emptied, a gang of professional burglars broke into the building occupied by a firm of merchant bankers. Their target was the boardroom. Six paintings valued at £150,000 were expertly cut from their frames. The gang departed without leaving a clue. Police began enquiries, but there was not a murmur from the underworld.

The losers announced a ten per cent reward, subject to the usual conditions, which involved the recovery of the property and the arrest and conviction of those responsible.

There were no immediate takers – until the telephone rang on my desk in the offices of the *Daily Mail*.

'Remember those paintings nicked in the City last month?' a male voice asked.

I had a vague recollection – the burglary hardly attracted any media interest. Yes, what about it?' I asked.

'I know where they are, but I need your help. Are you interested?' the caller enquired.

I asked why he had not contacted the police or the loss adjusters who were handling the reward.

'That's the problem,' said the caller. 'I want the reward money, but I can't go to the police or the insurers. You see, I am on the run. I am wanted by the police. It's nothing to do with that burglary and I'm not guilty of what the police want me for. I've been framed. But I've heard about those paintings and I know where they are going to be in two days' time. What I want to know is this – would you be prepared to give the information to the insurers and claim the reward and then pay me? There would be a good "drink" in it for you.'

My reaction to the proposition was an immediate 'yes', subject, I said, to the caller's agreement to my informing the police of the situation.

The caller was not keen on the police being informed. He stalled. 'I must know I can trust you. I have read that reporters have gone to jail rather than reveal the source of their information,' countered the caller. 'Can I have your word you would never disclose your source in this affair?'

'Yes – I must impose one condition. If you emerge as one of the burglars, or were in any way involved in this particular crime, my pledge to keep your identity secret is void.'

The caller said that this was acceptable. He proposed the first of a series of meetings. 'Let's meet, discuss the situation in more detail, before I give you the information. Meet me outside Mile End tube station in an hour. Don't contact the police yet until we have talked.'

I accepted. I gave a verbal description of myself to the caller. He declined to describe himself. 'I'll know you – see you at the station,' he said and rang off.

My evaluation was that there was nothing to lose at this stage and maybe I was on the road to helping with the recovery of valuable paintings from a burglary.

I waited for ten minutes, standing close to the kerbside directly outside the station exit. I was seriously thinking I had been the subject of a hoax, when a small four-door car pulled up. The passenger-door was thrown open. 'Mr Burden?' the driver asked. On my nod he said, 'Get in.' The traffic in the busy road was already creating a small jam behind his car.

I got in and the car was driven around and around the back doubles. 'Where are we going?' I asked. 'Is this tortuous route you are taking a bid to confuse me about the location? If so, you are wasting my time. Either we trust each other or we don't.'

71

For the first time the driver smiled. 'It's not that. I just wanted to check that you had kept your word and not called the police. I was checking that Old Bill [police] was not following us.'

He then parked and, as we sat in the car, he spun his story. Because he was on the run from the police, he had been staying with various friends who had criminal connections. The previous day he had listened to a conversation between two visitors to his latest secret address. They were clearly talking about the stolen pictures. And they had claimed that a buyer had been found by a receiver. The pictures were due to be delivered to the receiver the following afternoon.

I was later dropped back at another tube station, after we had agreed that the next step was for me to contact the police, and my mystery man (who for the sake of identification asked me to call him 'Arthur') said he would telephone me with details the next day if the deal was on.

I did not contact Scotland Yard, the main London police force. They are responsible for policing the metropolitan area with the exception of the City of London. The City has its own force. The burglary had occurred on their territory. As they were dealing with the investigation, they were the proper force to contact. I was soon explaining the whole situation to a City detective whom I knew.

We discussed the possible motives of my caller – including the obvious one, that he was in fact one of the burglars, who was having difficulty in selling the paintings and was trying to settle for the reward money as compensation. The detectives took the same view as I had myself – at the least, the pictures might be recovered. There was this to gain and nothing to lose. But they said the insurance firm would not pay out unless the man made personal contact with them.

Later that evening, 'Arthur' phoned back to my office as arranged. I explained the situation – that in the event of the pictures being recovered he would have to meet the loss adjusters for payment. Arthur paused, then asked if I would accompany him to the loss adjusters to verify his identity. I said that I would. We arranged that he would telephone me next day with the address. In turn, I told the City police, and they said that once the details of the address had been given to me they would obtain a search warrant. I was welcome to accompany them when they carried out the raid.

Next morning, on cue, Arthur telephoned. He gave an address: it was the number of a property and a road in north London. He added: 'Tell me after the raid that the pictures have been recovered and we'll fix getting the insurance money.' I explained that I could not call him as he declined to give even a number of a call-box at which I could phone him. He said he would telephone me at 5.00 p.m. at the office. The raid was to be at 3.00 p.m.

I met the City detectives who were going on the raid for a drink in a bar close to their Snow Hill station. The search warrant was being obtained by a colleague. When he arrived, three CID cars set off for the north London address. The detectives had already done their homework on the address. The occupant was a well-known receiver of stolen goods, I was told. 'It looks good.' The crew of one CID car peeled off to a road running parallel at the rear of the receiver's house. All escape-routes were covered. As I sat in the car outside the front gate, the senior officer walked with search warrant in hand up to the front door of the chalet bungalow. The door was quickly opened. The occupant immediately invited the detectives in. There was obviously going to be no trouble. An hour later the officers reappeared – empty-handed and long-faced.

The senior officer joined me. 'We've been through the place with a fine-tooth comb and there is nothing.' He was philosophical. 'It felt it had to be right. Never mind,' he said. I apologised and, feeling downcast, returned to the office.

The operation had gone sour. The fact that the raided receiver had even offered the detectives afternoon tea and was not going to complain was no consolation. Then the saga was to take a series of twists which revealed a little of the true world of the criminal sub-culture.

It began when Arthur telephoned. When I told him the police had drawn a blank, he exploded with fury. 'They have got to be there – I saw them myself,' he yelled.

'Exactly where?' I asked.

'In the loft,' he replied. 'Tell those idiots that you push open the trap door in the ceiling in the main upstairs bedroom. The pictures are leaning against the rafters immediately to the right.'

I told him the bad news. The police had been through the house with a fine-tooth comb. They had checked the loft; it was empty.

I left Arthur baffled and furious. He said he had his own enquiries to make, and would call back. Then came an astonishing development. Scotland Yard was making a press statement. CID officers had stopped a van being driven by a young man in east London at 3.00 p.m. In the back of the van the officers had found the pictures stolen in a burglary at the officers of a City merchant bankers. A man had been charged and would be appearing in court in the morning.

I could not accept this as being a remarkable coincidence. At the very moment the City detectives arrived for a search of the bungalow, Metropolitan officers, by pure chance apparently, had been stopping a van and recovering the pictures, a mere four miles away.

The City detectives who had been on the raid were not happy, either. I told them of Arthur's fury – and his insistence that he had seen them in an exact spot in the loft.

The City detectives decided to go into action again. This time an extra person was added to their party for a follow-up raid. He was the Scenes of Crime Officer – an expert in the forensic side of investigations. He was the first one in the loft. He took samples from the wood against which Arthur had insisted he had seen the pictures resting. Later, the samples were checked against the wrapping around the recovered pictures. They matched. The pictures had been in the loft. And they had been removed just before the search-party arrived.

The receiver was later charged and convicted for handling the stolen pictures. The burglars were never identified. And Arthur never telephoned again or tried to claim the reward.

I attended the trial of the receiver out of natural curiosity. He pleaded guilty but was not jailed, because Metropolitan police officers gave evidence on his behalf that he had been of great service to the police in giving vital information during investigations into east London gangs. This, as the judge made clear, saved him from being jailed.

Later, City detectives explained to me what they had learned on the police grapevine. Arthur, they were now satisfied, had been one of the burglary gang. But, while they were now sure they knew his identity, neither he nor his associates on the raid would ever be charged because there was simply no evidence. Unable to sell, Arthur had worked out the plan to try to claim, through me, the insurance money; and he was prepared to see the receiver arrested into the bargain. Certainly there is no honesty among thieves. But, as the police explained, there is little honesty among receivers, either.

There is an accepted system in some areas operated by a few ambitious detectives in which receivers are allowed to operate without fear of personal arrest. The deal – certainly totally condemned by senior officers – is that, in exchange, detectives are supplied with a regular flow of details of 'expendable' people who try to sell the fruits of their burglary operations.

It is an understandable system. The police, swamped by a tidal wave of crime, must make arrests. Receivers are key men in the chain of recycling. By their very trade they know the identities of active burglars and other dealers involved in the handling of stolen goods. So receivers are allowed to make money from some deals and in others, by arrangement, some burglars are arrested red-handed.

In this case, the Yard had decided to act and save the receiver from arrest, when they learned from the City police that an arresting squad was being sent to the bunglow where the pictures were being stored. The Yard men acted this way because the receiver was a valuable informer and they did not want him put out of action.

The receiver was immediately warned by the Yard that the City police were about to raid his home. At the same time, the Yard men could not justify the valuable paintings remaining in crooked hands. They told the receiver the paintings would have to be seized. A ploy was immediately hatched. The receiver would place the paintings in a van and pay a young small-time crook to drive the vehicle to an address on the other side of London. The receiver gave the Yard the details of the van, the time of departure from his bungalow home and the destination.

It was an easy matter for the Yard to arrange for the van to be stopped in east London. The paintings were recovered. The driver protested his innocence when arrested. He was charged, in due course appeared in court, and was fined. The receiver viewed the prospect of payment of the fine and giving a cash bonus to the driver as a minor penalty – he thought he was going to escape scot free. In this particular case the Yard's plan came unstuck. But this type of relationship is dangerous. However well-intentioned these working arrangements with crooks may appear, they can lead to corruption.

The Yard in particular no longer turns a blind eye to these relationships and officers' dealings with informers are much more closely checked. Some of these relationships certainly do still exist today, but the receiver is in greater danger, because senior officers now believe that the arrest of receivers reduces the outlets for stolen goods and puts the burglar more at risk.

All this is because burglary has become Britain's major crime problem. The police know all too well the size of this problem. They have very limited successes. In 1978 police in England and Wales detected 47,536 offences of 'handling stolen goods'. Many of these offences involved the proceeds of burglary, but the volume of arrests for 'handling' is minute compared with the staggering volume of the crime of burglary. The extent of the booming business of receivers forced the police to take some positive steps by the end of 1979.

5 The Burglar Detective

Knowing a man is an active burglar is one thing. Obtaining sufficient evidence to make an arrest and place the case for public examination in a court, with a fair chance of convicting the guilty, is quite another. A good police officer knows that to set out to obtain sufficient evidence against any one of the thousands of burglar teams is going to require a lot of time and dedication. Police dedication is without question. It is the time and the resources that are at a premium. Serious crimes, such as a wage-snatch, a mugging, or a sex attack, are happening all the time and must take priority. The average police officer has to fit in the chasing of burglars when and where he can.

There is no such problem for the small number of special burglar squads set up in particularly hard-hit areas for the duration of a set enquiry. They have the resources and are not diverted by the day-to-day events that occur at a police station.

A further discouragement for the police on the burglary hunt is that burglars do not use violence as a rule; when they are arrested they are (as a racing certainty) released on bail as soon as they appear before the local magistrate, given *carte blanche*, as it were, to return immediately to carry on their criminal trade.

The scene is similar to that of prostitution. The street-girls accept the occasional arrest as part of their 'running expenses'. The burglar has the same philosophy. Once arrested, he accepts that there is a risk of a small prison-sentence if he has a bad record. If a burglar's previous record is good, his crime will only elicit a suspended sentence. But there is a risk of being out of business temporarily – and that threatens a loss of income. So many burglars, once released on bail, go back to work with redoubled efforts. There is far more satisfaction in going to jail, or being fined, with a handsome bank-balance. Burglars who know their business do not talk about a few hundred pounds or even a few thousand. Anything over £100,000 is the likely profit on a good run by a two-man team.

All this is no encouragement to the police. But the police do care.

Many a dedicated officer makes time to bring just such burglars to justice – even if it means arresting and rearresting after bail.

One such officer is a detective sergeant based at a small Metropolitan police station at the extremity of the London surburbs in north London. One of his officers had a good break – two burglars had been spotted by routine patrol as they left a house. Once the burglars realised they had been seen, it was simply a case of – as the criminal underworld so succinctly puts it – 'having it away on your toes'.

The burglars' daily PT training was their salvation. Up and over garden walls. Through gardens. The same in the next road and the next until well clear. The police have no chance. But burglars do not wear masks or hoods; that is the gear for hold-up men. The patrolling officer had caught a glimpse of one of the men. Back at the station, a check of pictures of known and convicted burglars gave a lead. There was a distinct likeness to one on file. The sergeant took over and checked the criminal intelligence files held in his station. These list the known villains, their cars and, most important, their associates. From this emerged the possible identity of the second man in the team.

The next problem was finding out their latest address. As both men had previous convictions, the sergeant decided it was pointless to obtain a search warrant for their homes in the hope of finding stolen property. As men with previous convictions, odds were that they would have kept nothing from their burglaries that could be identified at their homes. If there was stolen property, it would not be evidence that they were burglars. Possibly a charge of handling or receiving stolen property and a fine in a court at the most – if it could be proved.

The sergeant decided to wait. Other jobs demanded his attention. But he tucked the names away in his memory. When he talked to informants he lost no chance of dropping into the conversation, as casually as possible, the names of the two men and a request: Any clue where they live now?

Just over a week later he learned the address of one of the men. It was time for a lengthy surveillance. The enclosed nondescript van, available to his station, was in use in the hunt for a young coloured boy who had been snatching purses in a local square. The van is fitted out with a chair, a toilet and a powerful spy-hole for day and night observation. The battered vehicle could be driven to any point and the driver seen to walk away – leaving his hidden colleague to wait and watch.

As soon as the mugger had been arrested, the sergeant borrowed the vehicle. It took two days before the suspected burglar was visited by his associate. A skilful bit of shadowing as the man left revealed his address. Now for the police the really serious work could begin: full-time shadowing to catch the men red-handed. Local stations can mount a limited operation. But Scotland Yard had a specialist department for just such a task – its work is kept as secret as possible. It is a department with the code name C11. At Scotland Yard all the specialist squads in the CID use the identifying code 'C'. It means Central Office. And Central Office 11 stands for Criminal Intelligence Department.

Criminal Intelligence Department

A notice outside the door leading to a suite of offices on the fifth floor of Scotland Yard warns: 'Entry only to authorised personnel.' The warning alone is surprising, because every visitor arriving at the single entrance on the ground floor of the tower-block which houses Scotland Yard, the HQ of the Metropolitan Police, is thoroughly checked. Security men examine police warrant-cards. Civilian staff have to produce their special passes. All other visitors have to 'sign in'. They have in turn to be personally collected by the person they have come to visit. The 'host' takes possession of the visitor's pass, which gives details of the caller and the reason for the visit. The time of entry is logged, and the pass is handed back when the visitor leaves. Scotland Yard is very security-conscious. Everyone – including the Commissioner – is checked in and out to ensure that no one without authorisation gains entry.

These main-door entry-conditions make such notices as 'Entry only to authorised personnel' at the office-entrance on the fifth floor surprising. What is special about those rooms? A small printed card denoting the occupants supplies the answer. It states simply: 'C11'. C1, for example, comprises the serious crime squads, which deal with murder, counterfeit currency, drugs, passport offences, extra-dition, bribery, corruption, etc. C6 is the fraud branch, C8 the Flying Squad, C10 the stolen vehicles investigation branch. But none operates behind such a security screen as that which covers C11.

C11 is Scotland Yard's real-life ghost squad. Detectives posted to this branch do not normally make arrests. Every effort is made to avoid these officers having to give evidence in court. All the men and women belonging to C11 go to great lengths to avoid disclosing that they in fact work with this branch, for theirs is the real-life world of James Bond – at least as far as spy-agency gadgetry and equipment are concerned. This branch is responsible for telephone-tapping, the secret opening of mail, shadowing, tape-recording conversations, and all the other undercover work that is best associated with the spy business. This department is totally separate from the Special Branch, who carry out similar operations, but in the political field.

C11 is the secret arm of the police in fighting professional criminals. It has been in existence since the sixties, but its effectiveness has never been so great or so much needed as now. It has the same problem as the rest of the police force – very limited manpower. There is seldom a dull moment for the officers of C11.

The criminal intelligence operation at Scotland Yard is one cog in a nationwide police machine. All forces, from Glasgow to Sussex, are involved in a constant operation in which information is gathered and recorded about both criminals and suspects who may not yet have convictions.

This nationwide intelligence operation works on two levels. It starts with the police constable on the beat noting items which may seem very minor in themselves – such as the new car-number of a youth whom the officer knows has recently been before the local magistrate for a driving offence; details of the van being driven by a window-cleaner new to the area; or the latest girlfriend with whom a local tearaway is associating. All this information is passed to an officer at the local station who is known as a 'collator'. The collator's job is to file the details and maintain an index for easy reference.

The second level involves officers from each force whose full-time daily task is purely intelligence work. This involves studying all the reports from local stations and identifying suspected professional and active big-time criminals. The intelligence department detectives then place these major suspects under intense but secret observation.

Extensive use of telephone-tapping is made in these intelligence operations. The Home Secretary in Whitehall has to sign the application submitted by a chief constable to authorise a telephone-tap. The key point in obtaining the Home Secretary's approval is that the police must state that to the best of their knowledge there is no other way to obtain the desired information and that they have very good reason to believe that the suspect is actively engaged in a crime which, if a conviction is obtained, will carry a prison-sentence.

The total number of telephones tapped by the police each year is an official government secret, but there is no doubt – and I write this on the basis of what many police officers have told me – that there has been a substantial increase in the reliance on telephone-tapping during the last decade. It is understandable and logical when, for example, the amount of urban terrorism is considered. The common complaint of police officers involved in trying to catch professional burglars is the shortage of telephone-tapping facilities. The Government gives a maximum allocation of telephone-lines that can be tapped to the various authorised agencies – the secret service, the police and Customs. The police, in turn, share out their allocation to their various departments. The anti-terrorist squad receives top priority. Next come the specialist teams of detectives hunting armed hold-up gangs. Finally, and last in line, come the officers hunting burglars.

Each telephone-tapping operation lasts for twenty-eight days. If the information being sought is divulged in a conversation early in the twenty-eight-day period, then the tapping is discontinued. If nothing of material interest is recorded in twenty-eight days, then police chiefs reconsider whether the telephone-tapping on a particular line is still justified. Each time one telephone-tap is discontinued there is great internal competition in the police force to take the line over. Well over fifty per cent of all major crime-arrests are provided by Criminal Intelligence – and the major part of this information is provided by telephone-tapping.

About five per cent of information that leads to arrests is provided by informers, usually crooks who tell all about colleagues to earn a lighter sentence for themselves. The balance of police success is achieved through sheer routine, hard and patient work.

Little wonder that the police are confident that they would be able to arrest more burglars if they were allowed to tap more telephone-lines. But the fact of life is that civil rights have to be protected, and burglary only becomes a police priority that warrants phone-tapping when chief constables launch specific operations against known burglars.

All really professional criminals fear being put under the spotlight by C11 – and that includes burglars as well as hold-up gangs, narcotics barons and protection racketeers. For when the Yard chiefs give C11 the go-ahead to put a criminal on its 'total surveillance' list it is usually the beginning of the end for the criminal.

The police believe that the increasing importance they attach to this surveillance is justified. Each month, senior detectives submit lists of men whom they suspect are making crime pay in a big way. There is no shortage of names of burglary teams which appear on the lists of suggested new 'target criminals' as they are called. Each month, Yard chiefs study the lists and decide on whom they should concentrate. The final list – a dozen or so people – is sent to C11. Everyone on the list then has every movement watched and recorded for the next twenty-eight days. A small squad is assigned to each person on the list. Detectives record the whole life-routine – how much milk is delivered, what time a husband leaves home in the morning, how much petrol he buys and where, the names of the people he meets and where. Many photographs are taken secretly –

and, if the police think it vital, they apply to the Home Secretary for permission to tap the telephones and open mail.

As a result, say police, the movements of major suspects around Britain are easily charted. The information is fed into a computer memory-bank. When one man comes under suspicion of being a big-time criminal, the computer can tell officers the names of his associates as well.

It was to C11 that our burglar-hunting sergeant turned. The dossier of his suspicions was sent to C11 offices with a request for a surveillance team. 'They couldn't have been more obliging – and I didn't have to wait long,' the sergeant told me.

Above everything else, C11 is good at shadowing. When the branch began, a detective realised how much the police could learn from the tactics of the government professionals. He applied for, and was granted, audience with MI5. The government secret service listened to his problem and immediately volunteered to teach him their arts. He was allowed to join that section of a spy-catcher's training course which dealt with secret surveillance. What he learned became the basis of the C11 police techniques of today. As a senior officer later told me: 'It would be right to say that once a C11 was allocated to shadow the suspected burglars they were as good as dead – that is, they would be arrested. If the sergeant's suspicions were wrong, and these men were not in the burglary business, then they would never know that they had been so thoroughly watched, and they would be cleared of the suspicion under which they had been placed because of the results of the local investigation.'

Only a few days after the request had been put in, a small column of assorted vehicles headed for north London to beat the morning rush.

The Hunt

The enclosed lorry – the size of a small furniture-removal vehicle – with advertisements for office equipment emblazoned on its side, parked a quarter of a mile from the home of the first suspect. Inside, it was in fact an office on wheels. On a desk was an enlarged street-map of London. There was a comfortable chair for a map reader – and close by on a shelf were maps for areas immediately outside the radius covered by the master map. A console of radio equipment linked the vehicle with every Metropolitan Police wavelength. The radio was multi-channelled, and if the vehicle was driven outside the London police force area the operator could switch to whatever frequency was used by the local constabulary.

This Monday morning, the radio operator tuned to the special frequency allocated to C11. The van was the control centre for a dozen officers who took up positions in the area. The range of vehicles was not surprising. They included a family four-door Avenger, a hot Mini, an MG sports car, and a small van advertising a window cleaning service; but perhaps most important of all were the motorcyclists. The riders of the motorbikes were all volunteers from the Yard's Traffic Department – total motorcycle enthusiasts. Motorcyclists play such a vital role in shadowing that each driver is allowed personally to choose the machine of his liking. Most motorcyclists in C11 go for the big Japanese bikes that can outpace the fastest of cars. The only drawback is the range – the bigger the bike, the more petrol they consume, and with small tanks and twenty-four miles to the gallon a refuelling stop becomes essential. But this is a small setback. In the heaviest of traffic there is no way a motorist can shake them off in a tailing operation.

In addition to the three giant bikes, a fourth officer was on a much smaller bike – the type favoured by would-be taxi drivers, who chug around the capital learning the quickest routes to destinations, a requirement of obtaining a taxi permit. He had distinct L plates and a high-vision red jacket. The 'all on-station' position was reached at 7.00 a.m. The motorcyclists, when reporting they had arrived at their positions, did not have to reach for the cumbersome telephone handset that the ordinary traffic policeman uses when he wants to make or receive a radiophone. C11 officers have the latest gadgetry: earphones and microphones are built into the huge space-style crash helmets that are so popular with riders since the law required helmets to be worn by everyone.

It was three hours before the action began, but patience is a virtue of C11. Waiting and watching is their game. The suspect was using a large and new Mercedes this time. His departure and direction were logged in the control van. The shadowing team swung into action. Only one vehicle followed behind for a few hundred yards. As the first car turned off, a motorcyclist with L plates took over. Whereas the first vehicle turned left, so the L driver turned right after a quarter of a mile. The suspect was already carefully watching his rear mirror. Nothing the police team did must alert him.

Shadowing is total teamwork. The C11 units work it out amongst themselves. Each unit has its particular dodges and tricks. But the operation has to work like well-oiled machinery to succeed. As one unit turned off, he would continue in the same direction along side-roads. He would relay each road he was driving along to the control van, and in turn be given directions. The order at which junction to take over the action came from the van.

The Mercedes soon pulled into the forecourt of an expensive block of flats. It was not that the burglar was ready to start work: it was to collect his partner.

The shadowing team regrouped, taking up fresh positions. The burglars had to be caught red-handed. On no account must the team 'show out' (reveal their presence). If the worst came to the worst, and the suspects were lost, then the same operation would be repeated the next day, and the next, and the next, until the issue was resolved. There would be no let-up, unless a major incident happened in town that required the team. All too often shadowing operations such as this one had to be aborted because of a priority crime, such as a switch to shadowing a terrorist suspect. But all was clear on the Monday.

The suspect was not long in the block of flats. His partner was ready and waiting. For work in earnest started at 11.00 a.m. They allowed themselves a maximum of four hours. Their secret watchers had guessed that they were a daylight team. Between the hours of 11.00 a.m. until 3.00 p.m. the most likely time for a house to be empty, the husband out at work, children at school, and the wife out shopping or visiting friends, maybe for a coffee morning.

The Mercedes headed for Hendon, and across the main road leading north and to the motorway. Then a cruise which took the vehicle to Barnet. The driving was impeccable. The speed limit was carefully watched. Soon came the first move. The lead motorcyclist sped by the Mercedes as it stopped, the officer reporting the halt by speaking aloud into his helmet. He did not have to take his hands off the handlebars.

The 'Q' van was next to drive down the road. The officer in the boiler-suit reported: 'They have disappeared behind a big corner house. The vehicle is parked and empty.'

The control van issued the next order: 'Units are only to move in if there is a report of the suspects emerging carrying goods.' One detective with a personal radio left his vehicle parked nearby and found a concealed spot where he could watch the parked Mercedes. No attempt was being made to find out what house was being 'visited', for the police knew that one suspect would be on lookout. To detain the suspect at that stage would be to abort the whole investigation. There was not a shred of evidence of crime, although the police had no doubt by that time that they were watching two highly skilled burglars at work.

Within five minutes the C11 wirelesses were busy again: 'Suspects returning to vehicle. They are empty-handed.'

The police would never know which house the burglars had visited, or what had put them off raiding the house. Perhaps someone had answered the door when they called, or an Alsatian had greeted their knocks by barking, or the house had been protected adequately with anti-burglar devices, but that was not the worry of the police. The tailing operation was on again. Hampstead was the next stop. Again the same routine was followed. The suspects parked quite openly in one road. Then around the corner. This time a motorcyclist caught a glimpse of the second suspect disappearing over a wall. He had gone in a flash – but it was enough to get the C11 team on top alert.

The team parked up – the getaway route was covered. Suddenly – too suddenly – there was action. Up and over the wall came the suspects – and they were in a hurry. They sprinted back to their car; but, again, they were carrying nothing. Clearly, they had been disturbed. 'Let them run – repeat, let them carry on,' came the calm order from the police controller. It had not been a good start for the burglar team. The police hoped the suspects' luck would change and that they would be successful, for the police could then guarantee a really bad ending to the burglars' working day.

The suspects decided to try their luck in another area. It was a long run down to Ealing, but there was no shaking those police motorcyclists. So far, the alert suspects had not a clue that they had company all the way. Every hour of a shadowing operation, the harder the task became to keep it that way. If the suspects showed anxiety that they were being shadowed, then the team would immediately abort – and try another day. But there was none of the obvious signs, such as repeated looks over the shoulder by the driver's companion.

Ealing is a west London suburb with its fair share of wealthy residents, and it is truly on the map of the roving professional teams. The Mercedes fitted the scene very well. No question of the occupants being a couple of scruffs. That would arouse suspicions. They demonstrated how useful the well-dressed approach was at their next call, an expensive block of flats. If there had been a porter on duty, he would have opened the door and ushered them in. C11 could not see what happened when the suspects parked up and walked inside. The police betting was that the men would go in and then out at the rear into the next block and try theft. But the police knew that the Mercedes was their 'home', and the wait continued. An hour this time. The suspects looked pleased. They were strolling back – no hurry. Maybe they had entered a flat and pocketed cash or jewels. But they were not carrying anything obvious. Maybe a friend lived in one of the flats, and they had been to collect the share-out of the proceeds of a previous day's work. It was still too risky to move in. The time was now nearly 2.00 p.m. Time for that day was fast running out. Would the suspects be returning home? If so, then it would be the same operation again the next day. But the route taken by the Mercedes showed that the day's work was not over.

Over Kew Bridge, across the Thames into south London, and into Putney. As the Mercedes went over one bridge, so did the police 'Q' van. Two motorcyclists were not many hundreds of yards behind, and the others were crossing the river at Richmond to take up positions in front.

This time the suspects appeared to have a specific destination. Into a smart housing estate. It made observation more difficult, but the Mercedes was quickly parked by a complex of private garages. Maybe the burglars had spotted a house in the same location previously. They clearly knew their way about. Up and over a perimeter wall by the garages, and into the grounds of a detached house. The police regrouped and took up positions. The van driver in the boiler-suit took out a box of tools and walked to a telephone junction-box as if to make repairs. A detective from the control van appeared, dressed as a road sweeper – complete with broom. He began sweeping.

Other units covered the road exits. Then came the action. The suspects could not have been gone more than ten minutes. The front door of the house opened. Out walked the first suspect. This time he had a set of golf clubs swung over his shoulders. In his hand he carried a golfer's bag; the police bet that it was packed with silver and small valuables. The second suspect had been lookout. The men were about a hundred yards apart and were walking separately back to the Mercedes.

The lead suspect with the golf clubs sensed the situation twenty yards before he drew level with the road sweeper. Maybe it was the two motorcyclists turning into the road that finally alerted him. But the watching police knew that the burglar had spotted the hunters the second they saw his body stiffen in a reflex action. As he threw the golf clubs and cases to the ground and moved to run, so the road sweeper went into action. The burglar did not get more than a few paces; strong hands seized him. But his companion had not been standing still, and the police were not close enough. There was no hesitation. He sprinted for a garden wall. A laudable vault and he was over. The motorcyclists were off their bikes before the wheels had stopped moving. Scratched paintwork and dented mudguards are not of great concern when you have the back-up of a police garage unit. Their priority was the fleeing man. But with their helmets and motorcycling clothing they had little chance. The suspect left them standing. The arrested man was handed over to the local investigating sergeant who had travelled in the control van. But he and the C11 unit had one more job before the secret back-up officers from the Yard vanished.

It did not take the team long to return to the north London home of the escaped suspect. They were sure he would return. He would be trying to work out what had gone wrong, the detectives realised. But he would not have the slightest reason to suspect that the police knew his identity or his latest address.

The escaped suspect did not in fact return home immediately. He vanished for a day, and it was twenty-four hours before he walked up the road to his home. As he reached for his front-door key two men stepped out of a parked van and made a sprightly reach for him.

6 Police Operations

Surrey

The growth in size and the increasing expertise of the organised professional syndicates of burglary gangs first came to the attention of detectives in the mid-1970s. The police were becoming more aware that it was not just a handful of gangs that were operating with great success but many dozens, maybe hundreds. One of the first police forces to examine the problem in detail was Surrey. The character and position of Surrey – a delightful county packed with good-class properties and a favourite commuter-residential area – made it an obvious target for burglars.

Peter Matthews, the county's Chief Constable, discussed the high burglary-figures with his CID chiefs. A special study was made from known facts in 1976 – and the obvious starting-point was an examination of burglars arrested. The CID under Detective Chief Superintendent Ron Underwood estimated that as much as ninety per cent of professional crime, particularly in good-class burglaries, was committed by criminals living outside the county, particularly in nearby London.

The 1976 study produced the evidence. For every one Surrey criminal arrested, there were thirteen who were resident elsewhere. A further analysis revealed that the vast majority – nine of the thirteen – lived in the Metropolitan Police area. The conclusion was that, as the figures of the study could only be based on those arrested, the real picture was probably that the proportion was much wider.

A second study then revealed that Surrey experienced the second highest number of dwelling-house burglaries when property in excess of £1000 was stolen. This study was based on figures provided from all county forces in the country. So in 1977 Surrey police knew the problem they faced. It was an extremely difficult task. They had to identify and arrest burglars who lived elsewhere, planned their

87

crimes elsewhere, and frequently disposed of the stolen property elsewhere – often before the burglary was even reported to Surrey police.

This presented a much tougher task: it is obviously easier for detectives to investigate and solve crimes generated and executed by criminals living within their own area. Surrey did have a special crime patrol. It consisted of eighteen constables, six of whom were detectives, rather than ordinary duty constables. All operated in plain clothes. They used three vehicles during sixteen hours each day, and each vehicle carried three patrol members – two ordinary duty constables and one detective. Surrey police area is broken up into six divisions. So each vehicle patrolled two divisions. It was a typical 'Q' car operation with each car free to operate with complete discretion within the two divisions to which it had been allocated. The unit had previously had great success, but the operation had been restricted by financial restraints which prevented the Chief Constable allocating more manpower or vehicles to the operation. Burglary was only one of the dozens of different types of crime they tackled.

A policy decision was taken to redeploy the Surrey special crime squad. On 2 October 1977, eighteen detectives, under the personal command of a detective chief inspector at police headquarters at Guildford, commenced an operation exclusively against professional housebreakers operating in Surrey. The old crime squad had tackled burglars. What was unique was that this was a major operation directed totally against the organised burglary gangs.

A special conference was held with the Scotland Yard Commissioner and his crime chiefs. Total liaison at the highest level was assured, for the Yard was not only keen to assist their nearest neighbours – they, too, wanted to learn what could be achieved in such an operation. London burglary figures were rocketing, and the Yard's detection rate was decreasing.

The Surrey special crime squad went into operation with multi-channel radios enabling them to receive and communicate with other police forces. The cars now could also communicate directly with each other. The Guildford burglary office was staffed by one detective constable who acted as a clearing-house for messages and co-ordinated intelligence collected by the unit. The remainder went out charged with the task of identifying and arresting professional criminals travelling into the county.

After early successes in arresting the first few top burglars, there was a fascinating development. As usual – mainly because no violence had been used – the burglars were taken to court, the case adjourned and the burglars released on bail. Detectives, convinced that some of the bailed burglars would be returning to burglary with

88

even more enthusiasm, launched a secret operation. While colleagues went to court with the arrested men, other officers waited outside. Later, when the bailed burglar was released, the detectives tailed the man from the court and stuck with him until the next crime. Often, on a second arrest, the burglar would be bailed yet again – but the police showed the courage of their convictions and set out to tail the crook once more.

In addition, the court provided much useful intelligence. To obtain bail the burglars had to call on friends and relatives to provide sureties (bail pledges). Often the burglars would call on the financial backing of other members of the burglary syndicate. The Surrey squad paid as much attention to the men and women putting up the bail as to the burglars themselves.

The results poured in. Between 1 October 1977 and 31 August 1978 the unit arrested 326 people, 226 of whom were resident in the Metropolitan Police district and 53 from Surrey. They also recovered property worth £224,702. Some of the arrested burglars had been caught red-handed after being followed from their London homes. Others were arrested as they haggled over prices of stolen goods with receivers.

But this is not the full story. Not all the people arrested were charged with offences in Surrey. Evidence in some cases revealed other crimes committed elsewhere. Most significant of all have been the Surrey police burglary figures. In the first eight months of 1978 there was a dramatic twenty-five per cent decrease. Chief Constable Peter Matthews commented that 'The redeployment of the special crime patrol has been an outstanding success in the prevention and detection of housebreaking and burglaries.'

Peter Matthews also headed a committee of chief constables determined at least to take co-ordinated action against the big-time receivers: many of the crimes commissioned by the receivers with offices in London had been carried out in their provincial areas. After discussions with Yard chiefs, agreement was reached to set up a special extension of the Yard's Criminal Intelligence Department. The provincial chief constables agreed to provide up to fifty officers to work with the Yard's existing Criminal Intelligence staff. The brief for the provincial officers seconded to the Yard: identify and then put under total surveillance the crime syndicates operating with bases in London and carrying out crime in the provinces. It was a limited programme – an extra fifty detectives against an opposition of thousands – but it was a start for the eighties.

Operation 1979

The success in Surrey was duly noted at Scotland Yard. The Surrey experiment had particular significance for Commissioner Sir David McNee. His predecessor, Sir Robert Mark, had organised in the early 1970s special burglar squads in selected local divisions. Good results had been achieved, but often the result was that burglars became aware of the existence of a local squad and simply moved a few miles to a new Metropolitan area where burglary was not receiving such attention.

Armed robbery had become the big dramatic and problem crime. Armed gangs had, Chicago-style, been roaring up to banks in big cars. Bandits had been rushing in with guns firing and swinging sledgehammers to demolish doors. It had meant that the concentration of CID manpower had to be given to this crime. Burglary could not, then, be the priority. Since 1973 the clear-up rate for burglaries in the Metropolitan area had declined steadily. In 1973 the clear-up rate was 17%. In 1978 the total number of burglaries recorded by the Yard for their Metropolitan area was 121,127. Since 1973 this was an increase of more than half. Yet during 1978 only 12,615 burglaries were cleared up – a decrease of 9% compared with 1977. The 1978 clear-up rate was a mere 10%. The rise in the number of burglaries in the Metropolitan Police area has undoubtedly been a public disgrace.

More and more questions were being asked by the media – in particular, why was the burglary clear-up rate falling so steadily at a time when the crime of such great concern to the general public had increased to such alarming proportions?

Against this background the Yard reassessed its position. The Specialist Robbery Squad was told to continue its good work. There could be no abandonment of the public to the armed villain, but the Yard's Policy Committee was taking a fresh look at the over-all situation.

The worst detection rate for burglary in the country. That was the alarming situation facing Scotland Yard, responsible for policing the nation's capital, in 1979. Even worse, the Yard was not faced with the highest incident rate of burglary. Provincial forces had larger problems but were solving far more.

At the Yard's annual news conference of 1979 reporters asked the Commissioner, Sir David McNee, to explain why the London rate for the detection of burglary continued to slide. The Yard conference was held before national crime figures for the previous year were published, so news reporters, at that stage, could only note that the Yard's burglary-detection figures were still going down and down. The fact that the Yard's record was the worst in the country was not then known. Sir David admitted: 'The clear-up rate becomes progressively lower as the value stolen increases.' The only real chance of solution was if the crime was solved on the day it was committed. Sir David reported: 'About 4% of those burglaries not cleared up on the day that they were first reported were eventually cleared up in 1978.'

This was evidence indeed that burglary had become big business with very little chance of the culprits getting caught. Sir David McNee was frank about his problems. He said of the abysmal detection rate: 'This represents a continuation of the steady decline in the clear-up rate since 1973, when it was 17%. Since 1973, although the number of burglaries increased by more than half, there has been no increase in the number of clear-ups. The clear-up rate for burglaries of residential premises was 9% in 1978, compared with 10% in 1977.' For burglaries of banks and retail establishments, the clear-up rate was unchanged at 15%. The rate becomes progressively lower as the value stolen increases. Whereas in 1978 18% of burglaries were cleared up, where the value stolen was less than £1, in burglaries where £500 or more was stolen the clear-up rate was 7%.

But the biggest sting for the Yard was yet to come. The provincial forces nationwide scored far better detection rates – often with a higher percentage of burglaries per head of population to cope with. Nationwide, there had been in 1978 an 8% decrease in burglaries. Sir Colin Woods, the Chief Inspector of Constabulary, reporting on provincial forces, did not mention the Yard's performance – the Metropolitan area is not his territory. He said of burglary: 'It is an appalling indictment of our society that in 1978 as many as 438,824 properties, many of them dwellings, were forcibly entered.'

Sir Colin, reporting the national burglary scene, also highlighted how bad the London situation had become when he said: 'The detection rate [for England and Wales] at 38%, shows a heartening increase on the previous year [36%]. It is a crime increasingly difficult to tackle and police look to householders to follow the elementary crime prevention advice which they are regularly given.'

The explosiveness of the London situation was not missed by the Yard chiefs. The Yard's policy during the previous year had been to tackle armed robberies as a 'top priority'. It had been argued that of all crimes it was the armed hold-up that brought major public concern and reaction. A Central Robbery Squad had, during the year, made wonderful inroads into the teams of armed hold-up gangs. But, then, the Central Robbery Squad had the personal direction of the CID chiefs, the best equipment and the back-up of utilising virtually all the reward money available for the police to buy tips. But compared with the total number of burglaries the volume of armed hold-ups – there were 734 robberies involving firearms – was but a drop in the ocean.

The problems of burglaries were discussed by the police committee of the Yard. This is a regular meeting chaired by the Commissioner at which his top aides voice ideas, and plans for the future are hammered out. Two key facts were highlighted. The first was that if the number of burglaries could be substantially reduced this would have a major effect on the over-all crime situation. Big reductions in armed robberies did not have this effect, because the total number of crimes involved was minimal. The second point was that, with such an abysmally small number of burglaries cleared up, a major drive in this area could also produce startling changes. The prospect of reporting in the 1980s big increases in the number of burglaries solved would have a major psychological impact on the fight against crime. With prizes like this in the offing, the only real problem for the Yard chiefs was how to achieve the results desired.

Assistant Commissioner Gilbert Kelland and his head of operations, Deputy Assistant Commissioner David Powis, discussed the problem in depth. The poser: Why was the Yard's clear-up rate so shockingly low? There were plenty of excuses. London is a special problem area. Burglars work the capital while living not only out of the area but also, in some cases, out of the country. Police officers argued that it was far easier for a provincial officer to solve a burglary. In a closed community the flow of information and identification of suspects was so much easier than in London. But this still did not explain it all away. An urgent enquiry into procedure was ordered.

The report did produce surprises. Because there was so much burglary, the system was geared for the fast processing of arrested suspects, rather than an in-depth look at each case. It was possible for a youngster to be arrested at 8.00 p.m., his parents contacted so that he could be released into their custody, and the boy back in the burglary business by 10.00 p.m.

The police probe also revealed that often a burglar would have committed several break-ins before being caught. The other burglaries would only be discovered the following day. Meanwhile, the burglar had been released on bail.

Basically, many burglars were not even interviewed by the CID. Uniformed officers, hard-pressed by their many other commitments, were processing those in custody as quickly as possible. It was this factor that the Yard chiefs seized on. The evidence strongly suggested that burglars were being caught, but they were not being questioned to find out what other offences they had pulled off. Getting extra offences to be admitted is a positive way of improving detection figures.

Many detectives argued that if they had charge of burglary enquiries those figures could be obtained. The burglars all watched television, experienced detectives argued. The kids knew that, if caught, the telly crooks could expect a grilling from the detective. The expert would be called in. There was a major psychological impact on the suspect, when a uniformed patrol man handed the suspect over to the specialist. It was a team game that the real police were not playing out.

All these arguments resulted in the crime chiefs ordering a major onslaught with a new approach. The new orders were that no suspect would be released until the next morning. Detectives would interrogate each burglar before release. A whole set of new rules was drawn up by midsummer 1979.

David Powis personally briefed all 3500 detectives. These briefings were carried out at major police stations throughout London. He announced: 'As a result of analysis of statistics affecting every aspect of residential burglary and its detection, it has been decided at high level to intensify police action in several areas of London.' The operation would be aided by the Commissioner's special back-up task force, the Special Patrol Group. The Special Patrol Group, often called the Yard commando force, has over the years been very unjustly criticised – mainly by political extremists who have clashed with the Special Patrol Group at demonstrations. Usually thwarted by the expertise of the SPG, extremists, unable to achieve their violent ends, have turned their assaults on to the SPG. There have been many unwarranted verbal and written attacks on the SPG. But, in fact, one of the prime tasks of the Group during the years has been to operate as a highly mobile task force, a key weapon against burglars. Of course, as the figures have shown, there are just too few SPG men to make any really big inroads against criminals. But they are highly effective when they move into areas where crimes such as burglary have reached totally unacceptable levels. In the autumn of 1979 when the Yard's SPG units were under tremendous attack, following the death of a teacher at a demonstration in Southall, these Yard commandos really showed their mettle.

But the quickly rising clear-up figures for burglary were not only a result of the physical actions. There were also the astute planning and policies of top detectives led by Mr Kelland and Mr Powis. In a message to all officers, the Yard's instructions were emphatic. It warned that the Commissioner and his crime chiefs were in no doubt that many persistent, systematic burglars were simply being allowed to be dealt with by the courts solely for the offence for which they had been arrested. In future, said the Yard, all burglary cases would be dealt with by the CID, who would take over full responsibility for the interrogation.

At a stroke, the Yard had taken the investigation of burglary away from the uniformed officers. No longer could uniformed officers who made the arrest then conduct the interrogation. The arrested burglar had to be handed over to the CID. There was cunning thinking behind this. Despite new career structuring at the Yard resulting in regular interchange between the uniform and the CID departments, plain-clothes officers still command more respect from crooks. Handing a suspect over to the CID gives a crook a feeling of greater importance and takes a little of the sting away from the fact that he has been caught. It's all right to be caught by a Starsky, but not by a flatfoot PC.

The next key Yard point was that no one in the police force must in future rush to prefer the charge – especially if the burglar was arrested at night – because the prisoner could well have committed many other burglaries or attempted burglaries. Many may not be reported until 9.00 a.m. when shopkeepers arrive to open premises and offices are reoccupied by staff. The police had found that overworked officers had been arresting suspects, charging them during the night, and then taking them to court first thing in the morning, leaving the police station at 9.30 a.m. for a 10.00 a.m. hearing. In cases of police bail, release was the same night of arrest. Now that cases had to be handed over to the CID, the detectives who would take over each case would not normally be starting work until 9.00 a.m. Half an hour was hardly time for the detective to evaluate the possibility of the burglar's involvement in other crimes.

So the price the burglar had to pay was a longer stay in police custody – all perfectly legitimate. It cut out, particularly, young burglars being arrested at 9.00 p.m. and bailed from a station by 10.00 p.m. – leaving them free to return to burglary.

In future, the Yard ordered, anyone arrested for burglary must additionally have his home searched – with the possible exception of a juvenile. Items that may be the proceeds of burglary found during search of a home could then be checked against details of property reported stolen and on the police stolen-property index. All this would enable the CID man assigned to interrogate the burglar to start from a position of some considerable advantage and strength.

Detectives were also instructed that, if a burglar elected to make a written confession, the arrested person should be told that reference could be made to other offences. If a prisoner was vague about details, the matter should not be left. The burglar could be driven around the district in an attempt to identify the scenes of other crimes. If such an attempt to identify other scenes of crime had failed, then in future the offence could simply be written down as having been committed within the Metropolitan Police area. The important point was that by getting every possible offence down on paper the 'clear-up rate' (the crimes the Yard could list as solved) could be dramatically improved.

The Yard chiefs also had the interests of the victims close to their hearts. Burglars dealt with at magistrates courts face a penalty under the Criminal Courts Act of 1973. This provides for an order of restitution or an order of compensation for any injury, loss or damage. The maximum that can be awarded by a magistrates court is only £1000 for each proven offence. If only one offence is charged, £1000 is the limit – despite many other burglaries being 'taken into consideration'. A very sensible instruction was given. Detectives, faced with a confession and a burglar asking for lots of other burglaries to be 'taken into consideration', now have to add up the total amount involved in the charge and the other crimes which are being admitted. Then sufficient direct charges must be laid, enabling the courts to order sufficient compensation to cover all crimes. The expertise of the Yard's crime chiefs ended overnight the well-practised dodge of burglars confessing to one crime, getting a maximum £1000 compensation order, and clearing their slate with confessions which they asked the courts to 'take into consideration', crimes for which the law did not permit compensation. Now sufficient are listed to ensure that the losers get a good chance of at least having legal compensation orders laid against the burglars. Crown Courts do not have the £1000-per-offence limitation, but this was an important move because so many cases are now dealt with by the magistrates.

Within four weeks of David Powis completing his 1979 summer tour of all the Metropolitan Police Criminal Investigation Departments, and briefing his officers personally on the new tactics, there was dramatic news. The 'clear-up' rate for burglaries had improved by 20%. Here, indeed, was proof again that when police concentrated their limited resources on a specific target wonders could be achieved.

But the 20% Yard improvement in burglaries solved has to be balanced against two important factors. The first is that the improvement immediately followed the stimulus of the head of the CID operations personally announcing his new 'baby' was burglary. The other was a fortunate pause – in fact a small decline in serious crime over all. The winter had really started with a vengeance on 1 January 1979 and had continued until nearly early summer. Nationwide, this had produced one spin-off – crime had fallen. Bad weather – particularly the thick snow and ice – had proved a most effective policeman. Criminals, from hold-up men to burglars, had not been keen to go into action, unsure that they could safely leave the scene of the crime because of a fresh snowfall.

Burglary in 1978 represented 21% of all serious crime. Coupled with the 25% represented by 'other theft and handling of stolen goods', the burglary industry represented at least half of all crime. Car crime accounted for only 31% of the total. Robbery and other violent theft – the crime to which the Yard had devoted so many resources – represented only 2% of the total.

The special squads launched against the armed robbers had

certainly achieved remarkable successes. In 1979 gun gangsters were on record as stating: 'It's too risky in London; we now prefer the provinces.'

The Yard's big anti-burglary drive can rightly be acclaimed as a success. But this must be balanced against the fact that the operation was launched because the Yard's performance against burglary had previously been the worst in the country, so any drive was bound to bring improvement. Even so the fact remains that the majority of burglars are never caught and most property never recovered.

However, any and all police operational improvements must be welcomed. The fact that Scotland Yard, Britain's most important police force, was able to make such improvements while still under immense pressures to cope, for example, with more public-order issues than ever before deserves praise indeed, but it highlights the issue at the crux of the matter. There are simply too few policemen. A complete restructuring of the establishments of police forces, with bigger financial incentives to attract more manpower, is the only solution. The public need far better protection – especially against burglars. The only way it can be achieved is with more police – from the beat to the CID.

Scotland Yard's policy of charging burglars with individual crimes so that more realistic compensation orders could be made was soon paying dividends. But in many cases the compensation that courts could extract from burglars remained only a fraction of the total losses.

The scheme applied to juveniles, too. The problems are highlighted in this case, reported in the *Croydon Advertiser* on 5 October 1979:

FATHER MUST PAY

The father of a 16 year old Croydon boy who admitted 51 burglaries was ordered by Croydon Juvenile Court to pay £925 compensation to some of the people whose property had been stolen.

The boy's total haul was said to have been worth about £11,000. As he is already serving a term in Borstal, the Bench gave him a three year conditional discharge, which meant his automatic return to Borstal.

The teenage boy's incredible haul totalled £11,000, but police calculated after considering cash and items found at the boy's home that the total that could be recovered was a mere £925.

7 How to React to Burglars

Burglary cannot be stopped. The incentives of high returns on the one hand and small penalties on the other ensure that the burglary business prospers and expands. So a stark reality of life is that the average home or business premises has little chance of survival against a really determined assault by a top professional burglar. But it is important to remember that the master burglars only select targets where there are known to be specific items of high value. Even here the burglar's instinct for self-preservation comes into play. As in the very large majority of burglaries, carried out by not-so-expert thieves, priority is given to the target easiest to rob. So a really huge area emerges in which residential occupier and businessman can do a great deal to help themselves. It must be accepted that the motivation behind prevention is primarily simply a selfish desire to retain what is your own. So by taking action you can push the burglar away from yourself to another easier target which becomes more attractive simply because it is more vulnerable and therefore easier to rob.

To remove yourself from the high-risk area of 'easy victims' it is essential, first, to analyse the method of operation of the burglar, and then to examine the whole range of measures available to achieve the object of self survival – from the simple and inexpensive to the most elaborate and costly.

The first step of this investigation in preparation for self-preservation must be a close look at what the professional crime-fighters – the police – watch out for in identifying burglars.

How to Spot the Burglar

Good burglars can be very sophisticated in their operations, and their expertise is constantly being perfected. But the large majority are not that clever. Burglary is too often so simple.

Excellent advice on how to spot a burglar is given to police by Deputy Assistant Commissioner David Powis. He has written a field manual for the police entitled *The Signs of Crime* based on his personal experiences of situations typical of those on which he offers instruction and advice. His book is a practical guide intended for 'ambitious police officers up to, and including, the rank of inspector'. The public, too, can gain from this. On crook-watching he tells the police:

> You can see thieves idling in all classes of residential district, walking slowly without apparent purpose, looking for houses to break into.
>
> Sometimes they call from door to door pretending to carry out repairs or gardening or to clean windows. When suspicious of window cleaners, see what they have in their buckets: water or air.
>
> Rubber gloves, like those used by housewives for washing up, are particularly incriminating if found in a man's pockets. If they are neither oil-stained, nor brand new, what possible explanation can there be?
>
> You may have a clever and careful housebreaker in front of you. In this context the wearing of outer garments inappropriate to the weather is sometimes a pointer. Many thieves are fundamentally greedy and even in midsummer cannot resist stealing a good quality winter overcoat in a housebreaking.
>
> A man or woman wearing an overcoat of good quality in a car in summertime, therefore, and people wearing a mixture of shabby and smart clothing, are always worth gentle enquiry. Learn the difference between expensive and inferior coats and capes. Sable and mink do not go with paste jewelry, tawdry make-up, cheap spectacles or sunglasses and low-priced mass-produced cars.
>
> Watch for the direct and incisively searching glance of the thief so intent, so concentrated and so revealing. This is the master key to recognising people up to no good. It should be looked for particularly when it is associated with an outwardly innocent movement, like picking up a glove.
>
> When in action, thieves' glances are either flinty hard (and once seen never forgotten) or at the other extreme are vacuous and dull. They wish to look casual and honest so in their play-acting they overdo it. But be careful they do not catch you watching them in the same way.
>
> Two or more men in an unlighted vehicle at night, stationary or moving slowly and suspiciously, are *always* worth an

enquiry. Note the car number – even in ballpoint on the back of your hand.

A car with engine running while stationary, with bonnet open and a man examining engine may turn out to be a getaway vehicle, so be particularly suspicious if there is another man sitting in either the driver's or front passenger's seat.

And do not be put off by the man sitting in the passenger seat. An observer agrees in his mind that a passenger *must* wait for the return of the driver. This rightful suspicion is blunted by a simple ruse. Do not be taken in.

How the Burglar Enters

1 and **3** A front or rear door without adequate security will attract burglars. This door should have a good-quality five- to ten-lever deadlock and, assuming the wood is more than 1¾ inches thick, a mortise lock.

2 A home is not a prison, but today window-locks are an essential deterrent. A slim metal bar running across the framework of the small upper window can stop a burglar.

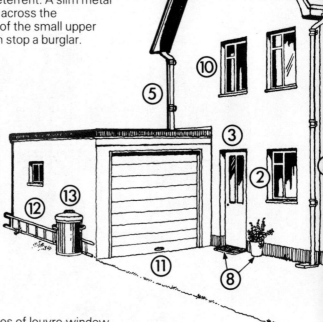

4 Many types of louvre-window glass strips can easily be lifted out of their holders. Unless the glass is fixed to the frame with a strong adhesive these windows are nearly as attractive to a burglar as an open window.

5 Drainpipes are viewed by burglars as a splendid aid. They can be climbed to gain access to windows or to the roof of outbuildings such as garages from where windows can be attacked.

6 French windows – even if double-glazed – must not be forgotten. It is essential that these windows have good door-locks. If not, additional locks can easily be fitted.

7 Letter-boxes. Make sure your letter-box can't be used as an entry-point for a burglar with a slim arm – door-locks can often be opened from the inside.

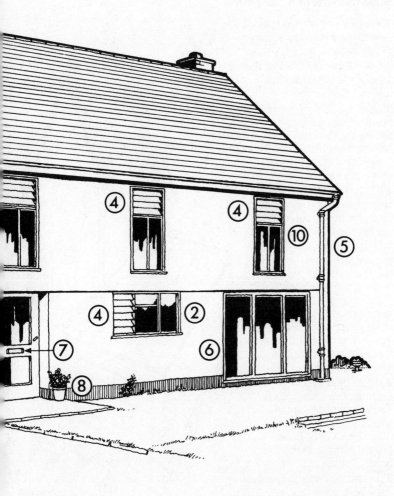

8 and **9** Burglars can be relied on to check under flower-pots and door-mats, and milk not taken in is a clue that the occupier may be out.

10 Upstairs windows must be protected. Window-bars and window-locks should be installed here.

11 Make sure your garage-door is locked. A burglar knows

garages often contain valuable tools. These can be either stolen or used to force an entry into the house.

12 Ladders left unsecured by the side of premises can be used for an attack on an upper window.

13 Even a dustbin can be used by a resourceful burglar – it's a climbing-aid.

How to Protect Your Home

1 Properly fitted modern lock – vital to thwart today's burglar.

2 Window-lock – easy to fit, prevents window being forced even if the main catch is released.

3 Window-bar – prevents slim burglar from gaining entry, and allows the window to be left open for ventilation while the occupier is in the garden or elsewhere in the house.

4 Louvre window – glass strips cannot be removed, because the occupier has sealed the panes in place with a good adhesive.

5 Always remove keys from the inside of locks when leaving the premises unoccupied. A key left in a door aids a burglar when removing goods: he simply opens the doors from the inside after breaking in elsewhere.

6 Door-chain prevents an unwelcome visitor from forcing an entry, and a spy-hole enables the occupier to vet a caller before even opening the door.

7 Letter-box positioned well clear of locks.

8 No key or messages under the flower-pot.

9 The locks have been changed by the new owner.

10 The top windows have not been forgotten in the security of this home. A window-lock and a bar have been fitted.

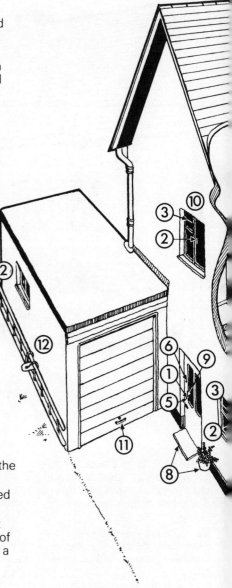

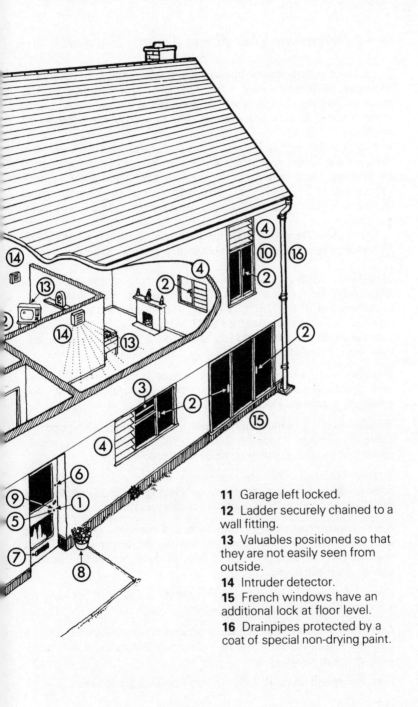

11 Garage left locked.

12 Ladder securely chained to a wall fitting.

13 Valuables positioned so that they are not easily seen from outside.

14 Intruder detector.

15 French windows have an additional lock at floor level.

16 Drainpipes protected by a coat of special non-drying paint.

Defending Your Home Against Burglars

No defence system against burglars can be guaranteed. In reality it is extremely difficult to stop a determined and professional burglar from succeeding. He will pit his wits and skills against the most expensive and latest alarm systems if he thinks the spoils are worth while.

Fortunately, not all burglars are like this. Many professional burglars are simply opportunists who rely on ease of entry and speed of mission. Here you can help yourself and avoid the traumatic experience of being burgled. You will not put the burglar out of business. Your actions will simply send him to other, less difficult premises.

For those willing to help themselves the following is a basic guide to turning a home into a reasonably secure 'fortress' against burglars.

Door-locks Millions of homes have locks on front and back doors that could be 'picked' by a child. Many of these locks were manufactured in the 1930s. Replace immediately with a lock conforming to British Standard BS 3621. Rim automatic deadlocks and mortise deadlocks are suitable for main doors. Fit one of each type to each door if possible.

Window-locks These are just as important as door-locks. They are easy to fit, and many varieties are available for both metal and wood casement-windows. Don't forget the fanlight.

Window-bars A home is not a prison. Windows exist to be opened, especially fanlight windows. A slim metal bar running horizontally can stop a burglar slipping in when the window is open.

Louvre windows The glass in many louvre units is simple to remove. But it's easy to alter this by glueing the glass strips to the metal-frame holders using adhesive such as Araldite.

Keys Always remove keys from doors and windows. Once a burglar has sneaked in he needs space to remove the larger items. Don't make it easy for him by leaving keys in doors which he can then unlock from the inside.

Door-viewer and chain Fit both and always use them. They can stop a doorstep burglar from gaining access.

Letter-boxes Make sure that the letter-box is not positioned so that a thin arm – particularly a child's – can reach through and unfasten a lock from the inside.

Flower-pots and doormats Never leave keys under either.

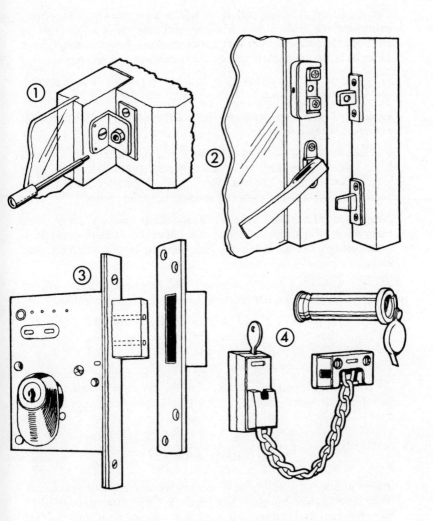

1 Sash window-lock
2 Casement window-lock
3 Mortise deadlock
4 Door-chain and spy-hole
viewer

Moving   Unless you are moving into a brand-new home, change all the locks as soon as possible.

Top windows   The ground floor is the area most at risk. After protecting the ground-floor windows and doors take a close look at the upper sections. Ensure that upper windows, however small, have locks or bolts – especially if they are near wall- or drain-pipes.

Garages and sheds   Always leave locked – especially if they contain tools that could be used to force an entry into the house.

Ladders   Chain and padlock them to a secure and permanent structure when not in use.

Valuables   Try to position valuable items such as colour TV sets, hi-fi, clocks, porcelain, etc., out of view from windows through which casual callers can see. Record serial numbers of TV sets, radios, record sets and cameras; it could help the police.

Neighbours   The best 'guards' of all when you are away. Tell neighbours who are good friends about your movements – especially when going away for a holiday. Ask them to keep a watch on your home.

Double glazing   A good deterrent – but pointless if double-glazed doors or windows are left either unlocked or with keys in locks.

Callers   Help yourself and neighbours by being alert for bogus survey callers asking questions about shopping and other movements of either yourself or other residents.

Police   Contact the Crime Prevention Officer at your local station for free advice if you believe you want further help or have a special problem. Also advise police if you are going away on a long holiday.

Security Devices

Every minute of every hour of every day a household is burgled. Insurance against burglary has been the key instrument used by house-owners and commercial premises to mitigate the impact of the crime. Burglary has bred another multi-million-pound industry – the security business.

Many hundreds of firms now sell protection. They range from the huge organisations whose shares are quoted on the Stock Exchange to the one-man guard who sells himself and his Alsation dog as a freelance nightwatchman. Today, they and an extraordinary range of products are being given the big sell to the public.

Some devices are straight from the world of real-life spies and counter-espionage. They are constantly being improved in a running battle with the burglars who employ equally ingenious devices to try to beat the traps. Here is how the James Bond type of anti-burglar devices on sale today work.

Concealed contacts The most basic of the security systems. The contacts are fitted to internal doors. The theory is that once a burglar has gained entrance he must move about the house. He is unlikely to remain in a single room. When the occupant locks up his premises on departure he closes all interior doors. Contacts on the door and the frame meet on the shutting of the door to complete an electric circuit. The occupant's last chore is to turn a hidden master-switch to the 'on' position. If any of the doors is subsequently opened, the circuit is broken and an alarm activated. Many people also have contact alarms fitted to window-frames and perimeter-doors.

Pressure pads Experts fit these pads beneath doormats, fitted carpets, and other floor coverings. They are activated by the pressure of an intruder's foot as he steps on the pads. This completes an electrical circuit – detonating the alarm.

Personal alarm/attack switches Thousands of homes now have these systems. They are always separate from other alarm-systems so that they will function whether or not other circuits have been turned on. They involve discreetly fitted push-buttons by entrance-doors and in bedrooms, and are useful if an occupant is in bed and awakes to hear a burglar in the process of trying to break in. These can either sound an exterior alarm or silently send out a 999 call over the telephone system.

These systems have become popular not only because of the growth of burglary, but also because of the threat of urban terrorists such as IRA assassins. Concealed contacts, pressure pads and personal alarm buttons are the most widely used devices and are now commonplace. Experts can fit a complete system for a few hundred pounds. Some firms sell and others rent out equipment on a yearly contract basis.

What is surprising, however, is the number of householders who are spending much larger sums to protect their homes and valuables. This particularly applies to upper-middle-class homes. As sales increase, so prices come down. Now they cost hundreds rather than thousands of pounds. These devices include:

Microwave detectors The microwave protector projects a very high radio frequency over an area to be protected, and the machine is

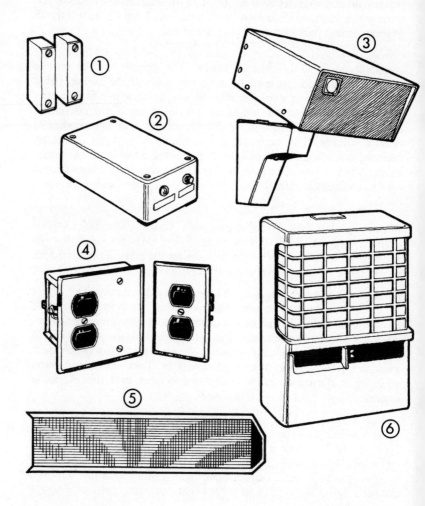

1 Contacts for doors or
windows
2 Personal alarm/attack switch
3 Microwave detector
4 Light-beam (invisible)
5 Ultra-sonic scanner
6 Infra-red detector

designed to evaluate the signals it receives back from that same area. In other words, the projected beam 'senses' all permanent items in the protected area. All the time the situation remains unchanged, the alarm is silent. However, when an intruder enters the area the signal pattern is changed and the alarm is activated. Units are designed to detect automatically when a minor signal-change is due, for example, to an insect such as a bee moving in the field covered by the ray.

Invisible beams   This involves the transmission of an invisible light-beam between two points. The range can be well over a hundred metres. Once set, all remains well as long as the light-beam remains uninterrupted between the two points. The light-source is gallium arsenide crystal, which does not have filaments like an ordinary electric light-bulb. Once the beam is broken – by, for example, a burglar moving across the path of the light – the alarm is automatically activated.

Ultra-sonic detectors   This involves equipment which emits a sound frequency far beyond the range picked up by the human ear. As long as there is no movement within the field, all is well. Again, if an intruder enters the field the alarm is activated. Modern Alarms, one of the major security networks, provides either single detectors or a master unit in conjunction with varying numbers of slave detector-heads enabling large areas to be 'covered'.

Passive infra-red   This is simply a unit that detects a change in the infra-red heat in the protected area. When there is a rapid change of infra-red heat – an intruder would produce an enormous variation – the alarm is activated. Modern Alarms say these systems are now very popular because the units are very stable and safe as, being passive, they do not transmit a signal.

So the selection of protection equipment available for hire or purchase is large. Yet a decade ago many of these detectors could only be found in high-risk government premises, such as the Ministry of Defence, where protection of the nation's top secrets has paramount importance.

Most of the detectors from the world of James Bond are designed to give the alarm once the burglar either breaks a window or door, or is actually in a room. But one firm has come up with an imaginative ploy to stop the burglar getting into the premises in the first place. This is paint that never dries, and it has proved so successful that the manufacturing firm has full order-books. It is particulary successful on drain-pipes – the traditional and still much-used access-point for burglars. Users simply paint the first six feet or so of the pipe with ordinary paint, then the upper reaches are coated with a matching paint that never dries. The firm rightly says that it has three deterrents. First, no burglar wishes to get a handful of wet paint as he scales a pipe on his way to a window. Secondly, the paint turns the drain-pipe into a slippery pole that is totally impossible to climb. Finally, if the burglar persists and contines to climb, he will come away with an item he would rather not have acquired – a coat of paint.

But what happens when the alarms are activated? Again great advances have been made by electronics experts. The triggering of an audible alarm – a siren or a bell – is the most simple. But there is now a lot more that can happen.

The 999 automatic dialling device　This is a relatively simple electronic device now very widely used both in homes and in commercial premises. When the alarm is triggered, a miniature tape-recorder goes into action. The device automatically dials 999 over the normal Post Office telephone network. The taped message informs the operator that intruders are on the premises and gives the address. The tape repeats the message several times. The main danger arises if a telephone at the guarded premises goes out of order for any of the usual reasons – such as a fault on the line.

Digital communicators　A further advance in dealing with the situation when an alarm is activated, the digital communicator transmits a coded signal over the telephone line. If the signal is not acknowledged, the unit automatically closes down – and tries again. This can be repeated up to five times. The decoding of the signal is carried out at area offices of private security firms.

The chances of failure are remote – but the security-consciousness of the public has led to the growth of an alternative. 'The situation now is that people have simply got to do more for themselves,' says James McArthur, Technical Director of Group 4 Total Security. 'Doing more', in real terms, means buying security to protect property because of the inadequacies of the police. Now the security firms, having cashed in on the business sector, are turning to the private householder.

In 1979 Group 4 set out to capture a large part of the private-premises market. They put out a 'budget alarm' pack, consisting of an alarm-bell, control units and five detector devices. For £25 a year extra, Group 4 provided buyers of the budget pack with a twenty-four-hour back-up service. It is a highly efficient and very good buy, but it provided further proof that the 'tab' for crime – and burglary in particular – is having to be picked up by the individual citizen.

Central Station connection　Across Britain a network of mini-fortresses has been built by leading security companies. Thousands

110

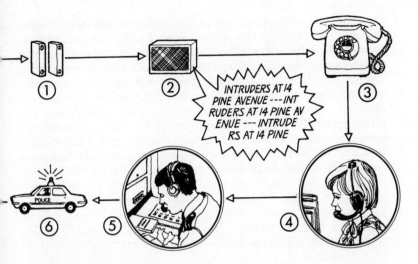

INTRUDERS AT 14
PINE AVENUE --- INT
RUDERS AT 14 PINE AV
ENUE --- INTRUDE
RS AT 14 PINE

Automatic 999 Dialling System

1 Contact breaks, activating alarm

2 Control-box

3 Recorded alarm-message automatically sent over Post Office telephone line

4 Operator receives 999 and passes to:

5 Police headquarters

6 Police car responds to radio message from headquarters

and thousands of home occupants and businesses have opted to pay for a direct burglar-alarm connection to the Central Station. The connection is via a rented private Post Office line. The benefit is that specialists man the Central Station twenty-four hours a day. They monitor all activity associated with the alarm system. The greatest advantage is that there is a substantial reduction in false alarms. For example, a false alarm is most often triggered by the occupant failing to carry out the procedure for setting the system either on arrival or departure. If the system is linked to the 999 system, the police respond by sending a car. But the Central Station operator can make a check telephone call. Subscribers are given codewords that they must use to satisfy the monitoring station that there has been an accidental alarm – and that a robbery is not in progress.

To study the effectiveness of Central Stations run by private firms, I visited a typical 'fortress', a most unlikely building in a main road in Peckham, south-east London. It is run by Modern Alarms, which provides employment for nearly a thousand personnel in its twenty-five branches. James Bond would have found it impossible to enter illegally. The control room is steel-lined. To enter the building the first step involves a front-door check. Television cameras linked to an interior monitor-screen watched by guards observe every caller. The electronically operated front door is only opened if the visitor satisfies reception over an intercom. Once inside, the security increases. More cameras cover the entrance to the control-room door on the upper floor. The first door is one of two, each protected with steel two inches thick. There is an 'airlock' in a small hallway between the two doors. Both doors cannot be opened simultaneously – and staff on duty inside watching the control panels hold the final trump card. They have a 'hot line' linked direct to Scotland Yard's information room, which in turn controls all emergency calls. If a gang attempted to blast its way in, a call for help would need only the time taken to lift a telephone. Inside the rows of terminals is the end of the line for burglar-alarm systems in houses, banks, jewellers', supermarkets.

The boom in burglary has spurred enterprising businessmen to cater for a real need. It has also produced a new first for Britain in the manufacture and installation of private security systems.

False alarms However, the boom has created a new huge problem for the police, manufacturers and subscribers – false alarms. The number of burglar-alarms linked to the 999 system in the Metropolitan Police area gives an indication of the size of the problem. At the end of 1978 there were 39,204 alarm installations of the type which operated over the 999 system. During the year only 73 people removed their alarm systems while 2420 linked up, and in that time a total of 92,928 calls were received by Scotland Yard. Of these, 120 were maintenance calls, but are included in the figures as they have to be answered. In only 300 cases were the alarms the result of actual burglaries. All the rest were false alarms.

A further 77,118 calls were received during the year from alarm systems connected directly to commercial and central stations operated by alarm companies, and relayed to police information rooms on a direct telephone line. Of these calls, 224 resulted from actual or attempted burglaries.

So the total number of calls received from the two types of alarm systems was 169,307. Not counting alarms set off during routine servicing, the total of false alarms in 1978 in the Metropolitan Police area was an incredible 166,153.

What can be done about this situation is a subject taxing the police, the manufacturers of the equipment, and subscribers. Certainly, alarm-bells that now sprout like mushrooms from hundreds

112

of thousands of homes, offices and shops have had an unexpected effect that has one far-reaching social implication.

The problem is noise. As the figures prove, so very many alerts are false alarms. While so many false calls infuriate the police, they drive the neighbours to despair. In some cases they have led to violence – neighbours have climbed ladders, cut clanging alarms from walls and hurled them to the ground. There have been fist-fights between angry neighbours and occupants of protected properties when tempers have snapped.

In the mid-seventies the problem became so bad that local authorities in several areas, besieged by furious ratepayers, had to act. The local authorities turned to the law for redress. Lawyers found that action could be taken under the Control of Pollution Act 1974, and the deterrent was fines running from twenty to hundreds of pounds.

An estimate by the West Midlands police is that each false alarm costs £50 to deal with, which means that the national cost to the public is staggering. The police, who have to deal with the alerts, are financed by the taxpayer and the ratepayer jointly.

A national policy that works with realistic enforcement-muscle could, at a stroke, cut down on much of this scandalous waste of public funds. Regrettably, only a little has been achieved since the start of the 1970s, and this by the National Supervisory Council for Intruder Alarms.

The Council has commendable aims. It was established in 1971 with the support of the Home Office, police forces, insurance companies and the security industry. The chairmanship of the board alternates between a representative of the British Insurance Association and of the British Security Industry Association. The Council has an inspectorate of seven experienced electronics technicians organised on a regional basis. They inspect installations, follow up complaints and investigate installers who seek registration on the Council's roll.

Initially it appeared that the problem of false alarms was on the way to being solved. The over-all objective of the Council was to improve 'the standard of service, equipment and maintenance in the installation of intruder alarm systems, and to reduce the high incidence of false alarms'. It established a Roll of Approved Installers of intruder-alarm systems and carried out inspections of existing installations put in by approved installers, using British Standards specifications. The Council also investigated technical complaints. But in 1979, eight years after its formation, it was apparent that the general public was not aware of the Council's existence nor of the help it could offer either to those with alarms installed by Approved Installers or to those thinking of having one installed.

Why the waste of police time and public money caused by false alarms is allowed to continue on such a large scale is beyond rational comprehension. It is all the more extraordinary that this state of affairs has been allowed to continue following the establishment of a council which could so easily substantially deal with the problem. At present the NSCIA is obviously inadequate to cope with the scale of the problem, but it could so easily be enlarged and made to work. All these years after formation, it still remains a fledgeling.

In 1978 Britons installed 7000 new alarms in their homes – a 12½% increase on the number installed in 1977. This is still a significant way behind the growth in burglaries during the decade. The NSCIA estimates that at least 750,000 intruder alarm systems are needed in Britain.

Personal Protection

A sixth sense – or perhaps it was simply a housewife's intuition – made Norah stop in her tracks as she withdrew her front-door key from her purse when she stood outside her home in Preston, Lancashire. As she said later: 'I just felt something was wrong.'

She had only been out of her home for an hour and had walked to and from her friend's home for a morning coffee and a chat. She had not walked up the main drive, but had taken a short cut to her front door by walking across her neatly cut front lawn.

As she froze in her tracks her brain registered the fine details of what had alerted her senses so quickly. There were distinct scratch-marks on the door-frame close to the lock. Someone had tried to get into her home in her absence. With commendable presence of mind she checked her next impulse to rush in and make sure her home was undamaged. Instead, she retraced her steps, walking as quietly as on her initial journey home.

Norah was ice-cold about her actions. She was in total control of herself – just as she had been in the hundred other crises she had faced as a mother bringing up a family of three children. The shock, she knew, would set in later.

Back at her friend's home she dialled 999. Within three minutes there were two police patrol-cars outside her home. They had arrived with blue lights flashing but no sirens. Officers were at the front and rear of the house while Norah's front-door key was used to open up. In five minutes the premises and outbuildings had been checked. The house was empty. It had also not been broken into. But there was no criticism from the police – simply praise. For Norah, using common sense, had obeyed Rule One in the unwritten book on self-protection from burglars. It is simply: Never enter premises if you suspect they have been visited by burglars.

In Norah's case, the scratch-marks by the front-door lock were real enough. A bid to break in had been made. As it turned out, her strong and modern lock had beaten the caller. But when Norah arrived home that burglar may have been at work inside. As a lone woman she would have risked personal violence – or worse – if she had rushed indoors and come face to face with the criminal. She obeyed the golden rule: If in doubt or suspicious, don't take a chance – call the police.

Norah's case was a situation with a well-defined solution. But in protecting yourself from burglars there are many situations where it would be wrong to lay down set rules.

Take, for example, a situation in the middle of the night. You are awakened by a distinct noise from a downstairs room. You lie absolutely still in your upstairs bedroom, totally alert, listening. You then hear another slight sound of movement. There is no doubt: there is a prowler indoors. What action can you take to protect both yourself and your property?

There is no set answer – just a whole series of suggestions. In each case it is the individual at risk who has to work out what is the right course of action. Step One is certainly to try to call the police. That's not easy, even if there is a bedside telephone and the intruder has not cut the outside wires. In the dead of night even lifting the receiver from the rest can appear to make a terrible noise. Try sliding the phone under the sheets, lift the receiver and dial 999. The number nine can easily be found: it is the second number from the bottom of the dial – the first is 0. Use two fingers, the first in 0, the second in 9. Dial, ask for the police, and then whisper, but clearly, your address, and say, 'Burglars – help.'

It sounds simple, but people who have been through this experience say it is not – and I believe them.

The police say that if you can't dial 999 consider running to the window, throwing it open and shouting for all you're worth. But this is only a possibility as long as there is someone outside who is likely to hear your calls for help. There is no point in this action if your home is isolated.

The key advice is to avoid action that puts yourself at real physical risk. What about having a go? That may be a solution if the man of the house is strong. But beware. A cornered burglar is like a rat in a hole. It is likely he will at least have a knife. Better to let him escape without immediate pursuit than to be knifed.

Increasingly, people who live alone or in isolated property are buying 'personal protection' alarms. These are a very good idea. A basic set-up involves a 'panic' button by the bed and possibly just

115

inside the front door. In the event of an intruder – or a problem caller at the front door – the button is pressed. There are variations on what happens next. Some alarms are simply linked to neighbouring premises, setting off alarms there. Others are linked to telephone systems, automatically calling the police. There is a wide variety of alternatives. Each individual has to make a personal decision – and that also depends on the particular circumstances. But remember – the key to personal survival depends on taking every step to avoid personal risk.

8 Private Alarms and Public Security

Former HM Chief Inspector of Constabulary, Sir Colin Woods, in his annual report for 1977, commented:

> Burglaries increased by 18% and it seems there is a limit to what can be achieved in terms of routine crime prevention. Unless homes are turned into fortresses, the determined burglar will have his successes. We are all very concerned, however, about the real distress experienced by victims when they discover that their homes are not sacrosanct and the unhappiness caused by this crime bears little relationship to the success reached.

But what can and is being done to protect homes and businesses from the determined burgar? Two services have a vested interest – the police and the insurance companies. In this chapter, we look at how some forces cope with the needs of insurance firms, burglar-alarm suppliers and householders.

A main reason why the burglary industry is flourishing without a huge public outcry is because insurance has taken the sting out of individual losses. Burglary has become big business for insurance firms. However, the system of replacing stolen goods with cash in exchange for a small annual premium has nourished the acceptance of a crime situation which otherwise would not be tolerated. The higher the scale and risk of burglary, the more millions of pounds of premium money flow into the coffers of the insurance firms.

It in turn provides work – legitimate – for thousands in the insurance world. Crime on the one hand and business on the other here become dependent on each other. The insurance firms welcome the growth of business. But it is true that, at the same time, they do try to keep their losses through payouts to an acceptable level, for their profit margins have to be maintained.

The insurance firms contribute to the prevention of losses in two

117

main areas. The insurance industry has crime prevention panels, and their experts serve on joint committees with Home Office and police experts. They also have their own experts who survey homes and businesses, where the cover and risk is sufficiently high. A requirement for these high-risk types of property is physical security – such as adequate locks and bolts – and alarm systems. Insurance firms want burglar-alarms to protect the property they have covered. But the success of burglar-alarms is dependent on a fast police response. Police, in turn, want to arrest burglars to put the criminals out of circulation.

Insurance firms and many houseowners want the burglar-alarm bells or sirens to burst into action the second the alarm is triggered. The advantage for both the insurance firm and the owner is that this usually puts the criminal to flight. Damage stops from the second that the alarm is activated. If the alarm is sounded while the burglar is inside the house, then he is likely to stop stealing and flee at once, taking only what is immediately to hand. But it takes time for the police to arrive after receiving an alarm. Too often, say police, the burglars are clear away by the time the squad car arrives in response to an alarm that has immediately activated the bells or sirens, in addition to putting out an automatic 999 emergency call.

The alarm systems work like this: the protected premises remain secure until the burglar forces a door or window. Usually this breaks an electrical circuit. It is possible that this can only trigger the alarm-bells high on an outside wall into action. But the most effective systems have a dual alarm. The circuit is linked to the alarm-bells, but also built into the circuit is a device which automatically dials 999. When the operator responds, a taped message calls for help and gives the address of the premises. When the two systems are activated at once, the police radio the nearest patrol car to investigate. The burglar is decamping at a fast rate. Usually he escapes and is free to strike again elsewhere.

The effectiveness of the burglar-alarm is dependent on police responding. Refusal to respond to alarms would mean the collapse, to a large part, of the protection system which insurers demand. So, increasingly, police chiefs are saying: 'We will lay down the conditions in future. You want us to dash to premises where an alarm is activated, then you have got to give us a chance to catch the criminal red-handed. There must be a time-delay between the alarm triggering the 999 call and the bells and sirens on the premises being activated and alerting the intruder.'

The police have also been forced into a new policy because so many alarms are false calls – usually due to mechanical faults or the occupant failing to follow the proper sequence of activating or de-activating the alarms on either entry or departure.

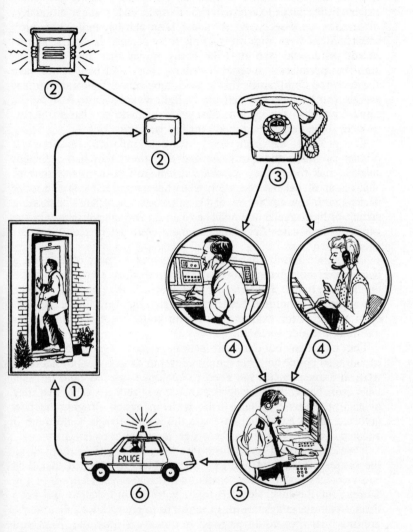

1 Burglar activates alarm on forcing door open

2 Control-box activates alarm-bell

3 Also transmits intruder-alarm message:

4 *Either* over private line to security company monitoring office, *or* over Post Office line to 999 operator

5 Message received at police headquarters

6 Police unit responds to radio message from headquarters

The Dorset force, for instance, found that in 1978 the number of false alarms reached 98.2%. The few that were genuine gave their officers little chance to arrive in time to make an arrest. Additionally, while they were receiving so many false alarms, more and more householders were wanting to link their alarms up to the alarm-panels inside the station. Like many forces they had permitted high-risk premises – such as jewellers' shops and banks – to have alarms wired up to panels inside the station office. When an alarm at premises miles away was activated a light would start to flash on the control panel in the station. Many forces made no charge for this service; some imposed a token rent for 'wall space'.

The problem has been that, owing to inflation, hundreds of private premises and firms decided that they, too, had sufficient value at risk to say they wanted a direct link to the police station. The result is that police-station walls have become more and more packed with row upon row of alarm-panels, each panel containing dozens of lights, each one relating to an individual property. On the surface this is a very cosy arrangement, but not in reality for the police.

The police found that they were having to post officers on a twenty-four-hour basis just to sit and watch those alarm-panels and the flashing lights. This became even worse as the police launched a centralised programme. Some smaller stations were not being kept open at night, for example – but the police were responsible for watching the alarm-panels.

The fact that burglary protection is such a growth industry encouraged police chiefs at national level to discuss the problem. All were in agreement on the need to cut down wasted time through false calls. Generally they agreed that it was very desirable that they police the volume of false calls with an action programme that involved sending warning letters to the worst offenders and then, if an alarm system was not put in order, a refusal to respond.

It was the issue of direct lines into the police stations that caused the biggest division of opinion. Some chiefs maintained that they had a social responsibility to maintain this service. Lancashire and Sussex, for instance, decided to stick to the old system and keep their direct alarm system, despite the problem of false calls, on the grounds that they could respond as quickly as possible. Kent and Essex took different approaches. Both have ordered that all direct lines into stations must go. Thousands of business premises and homes were given this choice: You go into the 1980s with two alternatives. Either you link up your alarm with an automatic 999 dialling gadget – and we will respond after the operator at your local exchange has noted the alarm-call details – or you link up with an alarm centre run by a commercial security firm.

At these commercial control-centres, private guards monitor, sift and sieve the alarm-alerts – and in turn call the police only on the ones that appear genuine. The police have encouraged this system by providing these commercial-alarm control-centres with a single hot-line telephone-link with the police headquarters operations room. If an alarm-light appears to be genuine, the private guard picks up the phone and gives the details to the police, who in turn radio a car for a check-out.

In the West Country, Dorset police have joined the forces that have been secretly adding another refinement. They have insisted on a ten-minute delay between a burglar activating an alarm which automatically dials 999 and the setting-off of the alarm-bells. The time-lapse depends on how far the premises are from the police station they are linked to.

Many police forces now circulate their policy to customers, insurance firms and alarm companies. This is the policy of the Dorset force:

> In view of the number of false alarm calls received by the Dorset Police, the following will be the policy in relation to all intruder alarm systems installed on or after 1 January 1979, together with existing systems in certain circumstances as outlined.
>
> The Police will only recommend alarm companies who have signed an agreement to abide by this policy.
>
> Response to alarm calls from a new installation will be conditional upon the system having been installed by an approved alarm company in accordance with this policy and with British Standard 4737.

There is little variation in the contents of the policy documents now being circulated by the forces. The main differences are that some have insisted that they will not retain direct alarm-lines to stations and some insist that there must be delays on the alarms to the 999 network and the bells on the premises going off.

Apart from giving the police better chances of arresting a burglar, the delay system has a big deterrent advantage – a burglar, while carrying out a raid, will have to work not knowing if he has already triggered off an alarm.

Several chief constables have now drawn up written policy documents which cover all aspects of installation and servicing of alarm systems. Basically, in this new policy for the eighties, the police initially require a security company to write to the constabulary's crime prevention department on receiving instructions from a client to make an installation. The police then allocate a police code number, which is incorporated into the recorded message which plays over the 999 system once the system is activated. When the system is installed, the security firm's engineer then has to present himself at the police station. First, he has to give proof of his identity to the station officer. The engineer then tells the officer the address of the premises which he will be testing.

These checks – particularly requiring the engineer to prove his identity – are a police precaution to thwart any attempt by a gang, burglarising a premises, to send an accomplice to the station and say: 'Don't worry about an alarm going off at "The Gables" – it's simply an engineering test.'

At the station the engineer then has to speak with the force control room to obtain permission to carry out a test, and afterwards tell the duty officer whether or not the new alarm is functioning properly.

Householders with new alarm systems are permitted a 'live' run-through of the procedure for locking up – and the alarm continues to sound on a mistake until they get the sequence correct. Police insist that inside the protected premises, near the control system, a card must be displayed listing the closing procedure, the opening procedure, plus details of the alarm company's service engineers. Because many false alarms received by police have in the past been the result of householders incorrectly setting alarms, police demand that engineers on routine service calls should also check that owners are properly conversant with the procedures.

More and more businesses and house-owners are turning to very sophisticated detection devices, so the police insist that the highly sensitive equipment linked to the automatic 999 system remains 'on test' for two weeks after installation. These systems are radiowave detectors, Doppler ultra-sonic detectors, standing wave ultra-sonic detectors, passive infra-red detectors, pressure differential detectors, capacity volume detectors, electronic vibration detectors, beam interruption detectors and capacity proximity detectors.

Invisible ray units have been particularly troublesome to the police. Now police say that invisible rays must not be connected to the 999 system until physical protection is provided that prevents accidental 'misalignment'. Police also insist that alarm systems must be connected directly to the power-supply, and be incapable of being turned off by a switch.

Most important of all – at least to the police – is the paragraph in the growing number of police force policy documents which states: 'When external audible warning devices are fitted, in addition to police call mechanism, there shall be a delay of not less than ten minutes before warning devices sound. In special circumstances, a shorter delay may be permitted.'

Then comes the question of the all-important keyholders. Police have decided that there must be a maximum of four keyholders for each alarm-protected premises. All must be on the telephone. And each must be able to reach the protected premises within thirty minutes on being told that the alarm has gone off.

Once installed with new equipment, the premises are visited by the police crime prevention expert.

The police have worked out a system by which they can get tough with the careless, the inefficient, the forgetful and the lazy, who accidentally set off their own alarms. It also helps detect poor equipment. It works like this: in the event of two false calls within a month, or four within six months, and the reason not being obvious, police deliver a letter from the chief constable. The letter states: 'I now ask you to let me know in writing by —— what action you have taken to prevent any further false calls. I must advise you that if you fail to comply with this request, police response will no longer be given to your alarm system after midnight on ——.' A copy of the letter is also enclosed 'for onward transmission to your insurance company'.

That final sentence carries a lot of muscle. For many people with alarm systems have had them installed as a condition of insurance cover. Without an alarm system which is acceptable to the police, their policy is void.

The person to whom the warning letter is sent is given fourteen days in which to reply. He has to state the action which he has taken to prevent any further false calls. If further false alarms are received by police while the offender is trying to resolve the problem of the fault, the police then ask for a meeting with the offender, the alarm company, and the offender's insurance representative.

The biggest worry to police is, of course, the number of alarms they receive over the automatic 999 system. The huge majority are time-wasters. So the police now warn that the police-calling mechanisms will be disconnected and police response stopped if after a suitable warning period (one month) an anti-false-alarm device is not fitted, if the offender fails to replace an automatic reset mechanism or ignores a warning letter from the chief officer. Reconnections after such action can only be permitted with the full agreement of the chief police officer.

Police who have adopted the new general policy also provide a full and helpful checklist for business-owners and householders who have alarms installed. Many of the questions appear obvious – but, as police and security experts have so often told me, it is the obvious that is ignored and sets the alarms ringing without need. Examples: Question 1 asks: 'Where any part of the alarm system is likely to be exposed to weather, dampness, corrosion, oil, heat, or adverse industrial atmosphere, have special precautions been taken to safeguard the system?' Question 41, which deals with electronic and mechanical wall protection, asks: 'Has consideration been given to non-criminal factors outside the protected areas, which might cause sufficient vibration to operate the alarm, for example: (1) children playing against walls; (2) industrial activity in adjoining areas; (3) vehicle activity adjoining the premises – for example, car parks, access drives, etc.' The questionnaire also asks people with infra-red alarms: 'Are receivers sited so that they do not face a strong infra-red source, such as direct sunlight?' And with space protectors – alarms that activate if anything moves within a set area – the police ask if the area is free from the presence of birds, mice, etc. Even the droppings of a bird have been known to activate a space alarm. With microwave detectors, the police ask owners to check that the areas are free from large reflective objects. It is possible for a microwave detector to 'see' items reflected by rainwater on roofs, or fall-out pipes, or even from Venetian blinds or fluorescent lighting. With ultrasonic detectors, the police ask questions such as whether the area is free from anything that can produce a large movement. The air being circulated when a central heating system starts up has been known to trigger off these devices.

All the questions sound very simple. But it is so often such basic items as these that result in false alarms.

Alarms have their different value. They offer real protection. They are here to stay and there will be many thousands installed in homes and business properties every year. The police welcome this. It helps their task in preventing and detecting crime. The only problem for the police is to ensure that the equipment that should be aiding them does not become an inefficient Goliath that swamps their machinery and, as such, becomes an aid to criminals. That is why the police are having to get tough – coupled with helpfulness, which is an inherent factor in the public service they provide.

9 Insurance

How much does insurance cost a householder? The answer is that it simply depends on where you live. Insurance firms have divided Britain into 'burglary belts'. The more burglaries in your area, the more it costs for coverage. The key reason for buying insurance against burglary is peace of mind during an epidemic of crime, with compensation in cash or kind.

However, compensation is not necessarily for items stolen – it will be quite likely that the payout will be for damage caused by an intruder. Many burglaries end with nothing stolen. The youngsters only break in for a dare, or are disturbed; or, having broken in, their nerve fails and they flee. Home Office figures for 1978 reveal that out of 560,109 burglaries studied in England and Wales nothing of value was actually taken in a total of 125,338 cases. Where cash and/or goods were taken, the hauls in all cases averaged £270, although a significant proportion – 124,353 – were only between £25 and £100.

There were 46,346 cases with a value of under £5; 101,042 of £5–£25; 114,534 in the £100 to £500 range; then 26,033 between £500 and £1000; and 20,122 between £1000 and £5000. The numbers decrease rapidly as the values get higher – these are often specialist burglars at work. There were 1603 raids with hauls between £5000 and £10,000, then 673 between £10,000 and £50,000, and 65 with a haul of over £50,000.

A large number of these raids resulted in insurance payouts because the victims had household content cover. Household content insurance also covers damage and loss from events other than burglary. For example, most policies cover against damage from burst water-pipes. In a really tough winter such as the one of 1979 the weather acted as a policeman, and many burglars stayed in their own homes, but the advantage gained from the drop in burglaries because of snowdrifts and icy roads was quickly lost. Insurance firms had a record number of payouts for burst-pipe damage – far more than they would have had from burglaries.

In deciding insurance rates for home contents the companies have examined other facts. Perhaps surprisingly, the highest rate of burglary is not in the south but in the north of England. At the bottom of the police league, and based on burglary per head of population, is East Anglia and the south-west. There are many reasons why burglary is more prevalent in the north, but police say the main factor is socio-economic, particularly the high rates of unemployment.

According to the Home Office statistics, compiled from 1978 police records, the areas most at risk from burglary are: the north; north-west; Yorkshire and Humberside; south of England; West Midlands; East Midlands; south-west; and East Anglia. But much more refining of areas most at risk has been carried out by the insurance companies. This is very understandable, because the major insurance firms which are members of the British Insurance Association paid out in 1978 an all-time record of £37.9 million to insured victims whose homes were raided.

As far as the insurance firms are concerned London leads in the Burglary League Table of Britain because the *value* of losses in London is greater than in the north – and the 121,127 burglaries reported by Scotland Yard for 1978 is no mean achievement by burglars, although not as high numerically as the north.

Some areas of London are viewed by some insurance firms as so much at risk that the firms are refusing new business. Most, however, cover themselves by charging higher premiums. So the higher up the league table, the more it costs to insure your home contents.

There are variations among insurance firms of the areas rated most at risk. But basically the belt is as follows. (These districts are from a chart drawn up by a typical company, the Commercial Union Assurance, which now makes public its views of areas most at risk in a bid to help customers cost their cover.)

Top of the league are the *London postal code areas*: E1 to E18, EC1 to EC4, N1 to N22, NW1 to NW11, SE1 to SE28, SW1 to SW20, W1 to W14, WC1 and WC2 plus Harrow HA1 to HA9 and HA0.

Second place: *Glasgow* with postal codes G1 to G5, G11 to G15, G20 to G23, G31 to G34, G40 to G46, G51 to G53, G60 to G62, G64 to G69, G71 to G78 and G81 to G82; *Paisley* PA1 to PA8; PA14 to PA15; *Chester* CH1 to CH5; *Liverpool* L1 to L66.

Third place: *Falkirk* FK1, FK4 and FK6; *Glasgow* G63, G83 and G84; *Kilmarnock* KA3, KA15 and KA17; *Motherwell* ML1, ML3 to ML6, ML20; *Paisley* PA9 to PA11, PA13, PA16 and PA19; *Bolton* BL1 to BL6; *Chester* CH6 and CH7; *Crewe* CW6 to CW9; *Blackpool* FY1 to FY8 and FY0; *Lancaster* LA1 to LA5, LA7 to LA9; *Llandudno* LL12 and LL13; *Manchester* M1 to M35; *Preston* PR1 and PR2, PR4 to PR9; *Shrewsbury* SY14; *Warrington* WA1 to WA16;

Wigan WN1 to WN8; *Bromley* BR1 to BR7; *Croydon* CR2 to CR4 and CR0; *Dartford* DA5 to DA8, DA14 to DA18; *Enfield* EN1 to EN9; *Guildford* GU1 to GU5, GU7 to GU9, GU11 to GU25; *Hemel Hempstead* HP1 to HP23; *Ilford* IG1 to IG11; *Kingston upon Thames* KT1 to KT24; *Reading* RG1 to RG12; *Redhill* RH1 to RH6; *Romford* RM1 to RM14; *Slough* SL1 to SL9; *Sutton* SM1 to SM7; *Twickenham* TW1 to TW20; *Southall* UB1 to UB10; *Watford* WD1 to WD7.

Fourth place: All other districts.

This particular listing identified exact areas; for example, if you lived in one of the areas in a high-category listing but not in the postal area mentioned, you would be graded as an area least at risk.

Variations exist on the burglary-belt chart. But what it means is that the higher the placement on the chart of the insurance firms, the more expensive will be the coverage. In fact, premiums are nearly doubled at the top. Example: some firms charge 30p per £100 for the areas least at risk. In our chart this would increase by 10p per £100 for those in third place, another 5p per £100 for those in second place, and an additional 10p for those at the top, i.e. 55p per £100 for London compared with the standard base rate of 30p.

Increasingly, insurance firms are insisting on better home security before they will provide insurance coverage at all. These can range from alarms to extra-tough locks. It is all part of the increasing price the public has to pay for burglary.

John

John, a thirty-one-year-old bachelor, is on the civil staff of the Metropolitan Police. He lives in a smart, detached, three-bedroomed house, built in 1926, in a middle-class road in suburbia. He has two 'paying guests', both girls. His hideaway in Surrey is far from being a den of iniquity. He is typical of the young professional, who has grown up in an era of sexual equality and liberal outlook. He is the 'father' figure in the home and outside and does not play the field. He has a steady girlfriend who works for the BBC, and the two girls living with him have never been an issue.

Working closely with the police in his professional life, John knows all about crime prevention. He protects his home with a Yale lock and a deadlock on the front door. He does not have locks on his windows. His philosophy is that it is cheaper to buy insurance than spend money on anti-burglar devices such as alarms, window-locks or other items.

He had not revised his insurance policy for years, and the contents

127

of his house were covered for £3000 when a burglar called. The burglary was only the first shock for John, for when he came to claim he learned that although his personal losses were only £410 – far less than the total cover – there was no payout of that amount. Like countless people who believe they are safe because they are insured, John was under-insured.

Basically, the total contents of his home were worth far more than the £3000 cover he had bought. The insurance assessor put the value at £8000. 'The insurance firm referred me to my policy and said they were invoking the "average clause",' John said. 'This means they assessed my losses in comparison with the total true value of the contents of the house – as I did not have anything like the real value covered, they only paid out £200. I was furious and I left that insurance company on very bad terms. I have reinsured elsewhere. I have now insured for £10,000 – more than the total value'.

Before examining the new insurance situation, it would be constructive to analyse his burglary. On the day of the raid our man from Scotland Yard had been last to leave the house after checking all doors were locked and windows closed. While John was engaged in his police work, a burglar had climbed over a side gate leading to the rear door and in the shelter of the garden fence chipped the putty out from around a pane of glass nine inches by eight inches. He then removed the pane of glass without breaking it and placed it by a dustbin, inserted his hand, unfastened the window catch and opened the window. Inside the house, he had worked methodically.

'Unlike so many burglars, he did not smash my place up – for that I am eternally grateful,' said John. 'He took only items which were easy to carry – items which had handles. These included the portable television, a transistor radio, which I had been given by my father for helping him out when he had a heart attack, and a guitar which Bob, a colleague of mine, had given me when I was best man at his wedding.' The £410 face value of the stolen goods was the least part of the haul. One of the girl lodgers lost £2000 worth of jewellery – irreplaceable, because it had been given her by her great-grandmother. She was not insured, and John's policy only covered his personal household items – so he had no redress against his insurance company. The second girl lost about £250 worth of personal items including rare records – but she was covered by her own policy.

'When I arrived home in the evening I did not immediately realise I had been burgled,' said John. 'It was only when one of the girls noticed a draught and went to close the kitchen window that the crime was discovered.'

John called the police and turned detective. He made his own calls on neighbours. Had they seen any visitors during the day? The only

128

slight clue was that one 'believed' he had noticed a Ford car of 'some sort' parked nearby. There were no other clues. There was plenty of advice. One neighbour pointed with delight at his extensive alarm system installed after a burglary and recommended it to John. 'It was astonishing; he began to tell me exactly how they worked and where the trigger-points were,' said John. 'I gave him suitable advice about keeping secrets secret.'

Because John was well known to his local police, the enquiry became more personal – although John stresses that he did not get preferential treatment. 'We had a couple of drinks at the end of checking over the house,' he said. 'I knew the detectives, and we discussed the whole problem.'

The only clue was a single fingerprint, but as the burglar was not on the police files the case will remain unsolved until the culprit is caught for other crimes and the print matched up.

'Of course I thought I might protect the place with window-locks and alarms, but I decided against it,' said John. 'It's much cheaper to buy insurance. I have now changed insurance companies and got a policy which is based on replacement value of stolen articles. It was not much more expensive than the other policy. I have also now declared my contents as being valued at £10,000, although the contents are today valued at £8000. After the burglary and the hassles of my claims, I want to be safer than sorry.'

The Home Truth

I have always insured myself against burglary. It has been a nice cosy feeling that, if the worst happened, I would be all right. Occasionally, depressed with the latest news of inflation, I have had the feeling that burglars could actually do me a service. If the music centre, showing distinct symptoms of wear and age, were taken, I could go out and buy a brand-new one. An excellent way of renewing the home.

Not that I actually read the fine print of the insurance policy taken out about fifteen years ago. The first cover I obtained was for £3000 – a fortune in those days. Several years ago I increased the cover to £5000. Renewal notices dropped on the doormat each September. It was just another bill to be met; the only inconvenience was that payment was due shortly after the annual holidays. Perhaps part of my lack of interest in the matter was because I had sent my copy of the policy to my bank for safe keeping. I had asked the manager years ago to add it to other family documents, nearly all relating to life assurance, which he holds. There was no point in risking the policy being stolen, or destroyed in the event of fire; much better to keep it in the bank vaults, was my thinking.

In 1978 I spent a few extra seconds looking at the renewal notice. There was a circular from the insurance people to remind me of inflation and soaring costs, and asking in the nicest possible way whether I was adequately covered.

I have never considered myself mean. The premium was only a few pounds. So I decided to raise the cover from £5000 to £7000. I admit the figure was simply a guess. If I had calculated at all, it was on the basis that a jump from £5000 to £7000 cover was a big percentage increase.

All was fine until I started to research this book. Never having made a claim, I did not know that insurance firms ever had such a mysterious operation as 'averaging' or that settlements depended on being adequately insured. My friend at the Yard really educated me about 'averaging' in payouts when he recounted his experience on trying to claim. As explained earlier, because he was not adequately insured the 'averaging' principle was applied and he got far less than the agreed total of the loss. It was a bitter moment of truth for him. From the many people I have spoken with, I am sure that there are countless thousands of people with insurance cover against burglary who have no idea of these pitfalls.

Prompted by the arrival of a renewal notice telling me that I owed £24.50 for the £7000 contents cover I decided to write to my own insurance company to check. The reply shocked me. The Service Manager of the Legal & General replied that my policy was not subject to 'averaging'. It was a straight indemnity policy and, in the event of a claim, wear and tear and depreciation, etc., would be taken into account. The sting was in the next paragraph: 'The cover of the above numbered policy is conditional that the sum insured shall be maintained by the Policyholder at an amount representing not less than the full value of the contents. Breach of this condition, i.e. a substantial under-insurance can invalidate the whole policy.' That really set me thinking. We had moved house three years ago and, what with in-laws giving Christmas presents of a microwave oven and a dishwashing machine, maybe that £7000 was a bit inadequate. We were not what I would describe as wealthy. The most expensive item we owned was my wife's engagement ring. At a guess that would not exceed £1000. There was a white fur coat (rabbit skin) and, again, replacement of this would be a few hundred pounds.

Still, I was perturbed. The insurance company had sent a leaflet issued by the British Insurance Association headed *A Guide to Home Contents Insurance*. In it there was a section dealing with 'Sum Insured'.

130

It read:

> The sum insured is the amount of money for which your home contents are covered and it is the most your insurers will pay even if they are totally destroyed, say by fire or explosion. Your policy requires you to insure your contents for their full value, so it is essential that you get the sum insured right and keep it that way. Some policies provide that if you are under-insured, claim payments will be reduced. So remember that if your sum insured is too low, you may have to dip into your savings to put things right.

Dip into my savings after the annual holiday! That made me laugh. But the warning-bells were sounding. I read on. The next section was 'Calculating Your Sum Insured'. It read (and I reproduce this item in full):

> Go from room to room, not forgetting the garage and shed, carefully estimating what it would cost to replace every item new at today's prices. For items covered on an indemnity basis (and some will be, even when you have a replacement as new policy) deduct an allowance for wear and tear and depreciation. For instance, television sets are generally reckoned to have a useful life of around ten years, so for each year of your set's age you could deduct one-tenth of the price of an equivalent new one today. But even this will be affected by the quality of goods bought and the treatment they receive.
>
> A wall mirror on the one hand is less likely to suffer much wear and tear and you may not need to make a deduction.
>
> Where it is difficult to establish the right figure yourself, e.g. for valuables or antiques, a valuation by an expert may be necessary.

In my case there was no need to ask the help of an expert. We have no Old Masters or silver collections. Instead, we have two growing children and a mortgage on a four-bedroom, two-bathroom detached house in Surrey.

By now I was thoroughly intrigued. What price the family goods amassed over fifteen years of marriage? How far out was I in my previous guess of £7000? Inflation was running high – perhaps 20% or more. These were my thoughts as I opened a notebook and went to the farthest outpost of my 'manor', the garages. In fact we have three – a single, to which a double one had been added by a previous owner on his acquisition of a boat. The boat had long gone, but the place was crammed.

A work-bench had been built in to accommodate all my do-it-yourself tools, and my thirteen-year-old son's 'hobby' – renovation of a twenty-year-old VW car – took care of the rest. Although my

131

son would not agree, I decided not to include the car in the house contents. While he would not sell it for money, I know I might one day have to pay to have it towed away. His sets of tools (presents for three years) had certainly cost over £50. That was where I started.

After calculating the contents of the house and garage, I was so staggered that I made a substantial inroad into one of my wife's seventy-two bottles of home-made wine (all maturing and not included in my pricing-list).

Many smaller items had been omitted, but major items put my worldly goods at about £20,000. I had a feeling of wellbeing until I realised that I was not covered by my insurance policy. The words from the insurance firm's leaflet 'substantial under-insurance can invalidate the whole policy' flashed through my mind.

How had my previous estimate been so wrong? By following the insurance people's advice and listing the items I got a realistic total:

Garage 1 Deep-freeze £200 (the contents are insured separately under another policy)

Garages 2 and 3 Son's car toolsets, £50; wife's shopper bike, £120; range of garden tools (spade, hoe, fork, shears, lawn-edge trimmer, sprays, greenhouse pots, etc.), say, £100; motor-mower, £150; electric mower, £30; sledge, £10; power-drill and attachments, £30; chainsaw, £50; tumble dryer, £100; woodwork do-it-yourself tools, £100; wheelbarrow, £10; Wellington boots (4 pairs), £20

Entrance-hall Cloakroom contents: gloves, £5; shoes (4 pairs), £100; 4 anoraks, £60; 2 macs, £60; scarves, £10; plant holder, £30; framed picture, £30

Lounge Music centre and two speakers, £400; 4 standing spotlight units, £150; settee and chairs, £1000; coffee-tables (3) £200; colour TV, £500; curtains covering huge french windows, £700; giant cheese plant, £50; framed pictures, £200; pots, glasses, etc., £50

Dining-room Table and chairs, £600; curtains, £200; wall units, £500 (contents of units – presentation cups, £200; glasses, £200; 50 tapes, £250: wine-racks and contents [excluding home-made], £100); best-quality Wilton carpets in lounge, dining-room and on stairs, £2000 (these are at risk during a burglary; if they are not stolen, they might be vandalised)

Kitchen Fridge, £75; Carron Capri cooker, £400; Toshiba microwave, £200; Kenwood dishwasher, £200; Hoover washing machine, £150; soda-stream, £25; Russel Hobbs kettle, £25; toaster, £25; Kenwood Chef, plus attachments, £100; iron, £25; Moulinex deep-fat fryer, £40; pine serving-trolley, £60; two dinner-services, £200; cooking-sets, dishes, pans, etc., £400; cutlery, £200; ironing-board,

132

£20; sweeper, £20; broom, £5; plants, £40; food, £75; roller blinds, £75

Bathroom 1   Roller blind, £40; mirrors, etc., £50; towels, mats, etc., £75

Bedroom (daughter's)   Roller blinds, £25; Venetian blinds, £75; curtains, £100; bean-bag, £50; books, £150; wardrobe contents including riding-gear, £300; dolls collection, £50; continental quilt, £50; covers, £20

Bedroom (son's)   Portable TV, £70; radio-alarm, £30; Scalextric, £100; bean-bag, £50; chest of drawers, £100; continental quilt, £50; covers, £20; pictures, £30; cupboard contents, clothes, microscope, cricket gear, etc., £300; spear-gun, £50; Venetian blinds, £100; curtains, £150

Study   Table and four chairs, £200; bed, £100; typewriter, £100; Kirby vacuum cleaner, £300; set of cases, £150; wall units with reference books, etc., £1000; curtains, £100. Cupboard contents: frame tent, £300; camping-gear including gas-stove, etc., £150; towels, spare curtains, etc., £150

Bathroom 2   mats, towels, £75; scales, £10; mirrors, etc., £100; net curtains, £5; roller blind, £30

Master Bedroom   Curtains, £100; bed, £200; bean-bag, £50; Teas-maid, £30; jewellery, £100; engagement ring, £1000; clothes belonging to self and wife in fitted wardrobes, £500; fur coat, £300; sheepskin coat, £200; continental quilt and covers, £100; dressing-table, £100; bedside table, £25; clothes-basket, £25; framed wall-pictures, £100; best-quality carpet-tiles in three bedrooms and the study, £750

All this adds up to £20,000 plus. Next, what action to take? I now knew of the two types of cover available – indemnity and replacement as new. The insurance leaflet was again helpful:

> If you insure on an indemnity basis, you will be paid the cost of rapairing damaged articles or of replacing what has been stolen or destroyed, less an amount for wear, tear and depreciation.
>
> For items covered on a replacement-as-new basis, you will be paid the full cost for repairs if they are damaged or the cost of replacing them with equivalent new articles if they are stolen or destroyed.
>
> Furniture, carpets, domestic appliances, televisions, radios and similar equipment can normally be insured on a replacement-as-new basis, but clothing and household linen cannot.

In addition, there was an index-linking endorsement available to keep the sum insured in line with inflation.

The insurance company warned that, while this index-linking kept the value of contents abreast with latest price-increases, it did not take into account cost of new items purchased after the policy was issued.

What was all this going to cost me? The present bill for the £7000 cover was £24.50 – money which would have been completely wasted because the total was so inadequate. The news was not so bad. In my case the additional premium for index-linking was 50p per £1000 insured. This, on the £7000 cover, brought the total premium to £28.

I wrote an urgent letter to the insurance company. 'Please quote for an "as new policy" with £20,000 cover plus a quote for index-linking.' I also asked whether insurance companies covering burglary gave bonuses for 'no claims'? I explained that I had never claimed in all those years I was insured. My car policy provided handsome 'no claim' bonuses, which encouraged me not to claim and to take special care of my vehicle. This would be good for me and the insurance company in the event of burglary. So why not?

The Legal & General replied promptly to my letter advising them that I had costed my home contents and had arrived at a total of about £20,000. Their service office manager wrote: 'The annual premium for a total sum insured of £20,000 would be £79.54 on a "reinstatement as-new policy" and index-linked on an indemnity basis the annual premium would be £69.50. We would advise you, however, that for a sum insured of this size a survey of your premises will be required. We very much regret to advise you that we do not give a no-claims bonus for household business.'

It seemed no longer worth while insuring. My declaration to the insurance firm had increased the premium of £24.50 for £7000 indemnity cover to either £79.54 or £69.50. In both cases it was well over a hundred per cent increase. 'I'll buy a few more window-locks – I can save on this,' I told my wife. She said, more prudently, 'I still think it's good value. New for old is a good offer – and there is a lot of money at stake.'

The letter from the insurance firm made no mention of bed linen, etc., that I had mentioned in my letter to them. I had guessed this at a valuation of £2000. I understood insurance did not give full replacement cover of such items, and some clothes more than a couple of years old might not be covered.

We compromised. I sent an urgent message to the insurance company asking for a visit from their surveyor.

I now felt very naked. For the first time in my married life I was not covered by insurance, and now burglary took on a more realistic hue. I had always taken sensible precautions – like checking that the doors and windows were locked before I left the house – but I had

134

bought peace of mind with insurance; it was the carrot leading me to a cash payment for any losses or damage and cushioning the blow of being robbed.

I was very concerned now. I re-examined window-locks – they worked, but the locking key had been lost years ago and not left by the previous owner. Some upstairs windows did not have window-locks at all. Whatever happened with the insurance, I would rectify these matters immediately.

As the days passed and I waited for a reply from the insurance firm, I realised I was 'hooked' on being covered. I realised that the premium, which at first had surprised me, was in fact reasonable when considered against the total cover provided. There were still warts; I felt strongly that all insurance companies should offer 'no claims' bonuses for household content policies. I could, of course, have shopped around in a bid to find a firm that might offer this incentive. But I had been with the Legal & General for years and I was pleased with their informative correspondence.

Most important of all, my in-depth research into the burglary business had convinced me that the risk was so great I could not afford *not* to be insured. I could have refused to pay the premium, but that would have been a totally false 'saving'. My peace of mind alone was worth every penny. The police (whom I also help fund through taxes and rates) are simply not able to provide the level of protection I desire. It is a regrettable fact of life, but by making a once-a-year insurance payment I feel I have, by financial means at least, repressed the threat of burglary with its attendant problems.

Within days of the insurance firm's reply the whole issue was settled. They were arranging a survey but pointed out that, owing to the proximity of the policy's renewal date, it would be best to forward the £24.50 premium for the existing £7000 cover. They said this would enable them to hold cover for the higher amount. Subject to satisfactory survey, I would then be invoiced for the balance.

They told me that bed linen, curtains, clothing, etc., were covered under the contents section and the value included in the sum insured. But reinstatement as new did not cover articles of clothing, wearing-apparel and household linen more than two years old, and an allowance for wear, tear, depreciation, etc., should be made when estimating the value. I discussed this with my wife. We had valued all items 'as new'. Based on our list, we guessed at a new sum and opted for the round figure of £15,000. I then immediately sent off by first-class post the premium requested.

Capitalising on Insurance

While the rate of burglary has been increasing, so, too, have the premiums of insurance companies. Insurance firms have had to increase on two fronts. The first is due to inflation – higher staff salaries and the increasing value of goods protected by their insurance cover. The second front involves all those clients who live in areas most likely to be burglarised.

Most insurance firms now have well-defined 'very high-risk areas', 'high-risk areas' and 'safe districts'. People living in a high-risk area pay about fifty per cent more than the standard rate. Those living in very high-risk areas pay about double. There is a tremendous variation in the prices quoted by various insurance firms for cover in high-risk areas, but it is not unusual for clients to receive bills (at the end of 1979) for between £5 and £7 per £1000 cover on indemnity or from £6 to £10 on 'new for old' policies. All this raises the serious question of whether it is really worth while insuring at all. As my own case demonstrated, it is not hard to price house contents at £20,000 – and run up a substantial bill for cover.

There is no doubt that insurance firms do offer an excellent service, including peace of mind, and there are now so many that it pays to shop around. But a situation has now been reached when it is valid to ask: would it make more sense to spend the annual insurance premium on anti-burglar gadgetry? There are now many cases when the answer would be 'yes'. A positive encouragement to turn from insurance to protective measures has, in fact, been given by a few insurance companies themselves. Some companies refuse to accept 'new business' in very high-risk areas.

The rate you pay for house contents cover differs with each firm because there are great variations in the cover offered. The type of job you have is also a factor. For example, one of the cheapest policies offered is by the National Farmers' Union, but this is available only to NFU members and their families. Some insurance firms give discounts – the clergy qualify with one firm, and members of organisations, such as the National Union of Teachers, the police, civil servants and NALGO members can get competitive rates. But the question remains: is it all worth it?

Certainly most policies protect against other calamities, such as fire or flood from burst pipes, in addition to burglary. Even so, with premiums at such a high level in some areas, owing mainly to burglary, the possibility of opting for the purchase of anti-theft equipment as an alternative rates serious consideration, and is actively encouraged by some firms who will not take on new clients in the burglary danger-zones.

Exactly how much is made each year from the burglary business is impossible to state. A conservative estimate is that profits for the crooks in the business, in all sections, exceeds £100 million. An indicator to known losses is the annual report of the British Insurance Association. In 1978, for example, the losses from private homes rose by 25% – from £30.3 million to £37.9 million. This represented a rise of more than twice the rate of inflation.

Mr Pat Bartrum, Chairman of the British Insurance Association Crime Prevention Panel, commenting on these figures, said: 'Thefts from private households now average more than £100,000 a day, seven days a week. Although insurance policies pay these claims, the total cost has to be reflected in the premiums. In addition, the contents of many homes are inadequately covered by insurance or not insured at all. The way to bring the mounting costs of those thefts under control is for everyone to take simple precautions. It is common sense for all of us to put adequate locks on doors and windows and use them. Insurance companies and the police are ready to advise on security if people ask.'

But these figures prove how the insurance world has done quite well legitimately on the problems of burglary. In 1974, household losses from burglary were £13.6 million – and that was in a year when there was a huge 43% increase. But four years later, in 1978, the losses hit £37.9 million. However, household losses are not the whole story. Insurance firms are businesses and, like all good business enterprises, they build in a profit margin when deciding the cost of the service they offer. Little wonder insurance is expanding with firms making healthy profits. Theft losses at commercial and industrial premises covered by the BIA members increased from £5.4 million in 1974 to £18.3 million in 1978.

A key reason why insured theft losses at industrial premises have been contained, far more than in private households, is because firms have spent far more on security. Sophisticated alarm-systems, security patrols and dogs have all contributed to keeping insured losses down. The BIA's Mr Pat Bartrum comments: 'We welcome the improvements in security which are being made in a number of high-risk businesses. Nonetheless, losses in the commercial sector are still substantial. Criminals are increasingly turning their attention to small shops, factories and offices. Businessmen, generally, just as much as householders, need to realise the paramount importance of proper security and to recognise that major theft losses do not always happen to someone else.'

Some insurance experts estimate that at least a quarter of the occupants of private property are not insured. Others are insured with firms which are not members of the BIA. But the BIA does represent the major insurance organisations and, while their figures are not the whole picture, they do indicate the general trend.

10 Conclusions

Let us now consider the burglary business as a whole and some possible solutions. Burglars have a better-than-equal chance of never being caught at all – the police 'clear-up' rate in England and Wales has in the last decade not even reached 40%. In recent years it has hovered just over 30%.

What happens to those few burglars who *do* get caught? It is a matter of even greater public concern that the large majority of those arrested are immediately given bail. There is overwhelming evidence from case-histories and police experience that many, particularly the hard-core 'professionals', use their freedom to carry on burglarising. They set out to build up their bank-balances and are not greatly inconvenienced by spending time on trial. Many who fear they may be sent to jail for some time are inspired to 'work' harder to add to their account.

If we examine the official Home Office *Criminal Statistics England and Wales 1978*, we see that in 1978 police in 19,600 cases rated the offence of burglary so low that they issued summonses after considering the report of the investigating officer. These cases were initially dealt with on the same basis as that of a motorist who commits a minor motoring infringement. Having been summoned, it is reasonable to expect the burglars to turn up at court – but 262 did not. There were 41,000 who, after being questioned as suspected burglars by officers, were later released from the police station on 'police bail'. They were free but under orders to report back on a set date. Of these, 935 failed to appear.

Thousands of suspected burglars are dealt with on no stronger terms than would be an offending motorist. Surely this is an odious comparison. Burglary in any form is a criminal offence. The fact that it is so prevalent should not signify it is commonplace, thus undermining its seriousness.

Stage 2 involves the accused appearing at a magistrates court. There were 78,300 suspects before magistrates. Of these 19,600 appeared in answer to a summons; the remainder were taken direct to court following arrest and police charge. Of the 78,300, 41,000 were released on bail. This means that 25% were summoned, 52% were released on bail and only 23% held in custody prior to their first scheduled court appearance.

Then the actual proceedings. Of 39,700 proceeded against at magistrates courts, 27,500 were on bail throughout their hearing. How many out on bail were carrying on burglarising is not known. There is evidence that, with only a 32% chance of getting caught, there are quite a few.

In 1978 there were 4000 convicted burglars sent to Crown Court for sentencing because magistrates felt the case required the greater sentencing-power of the higher court. Yet 900 burglars, or 22%, were then released on bail to await the tougher sentences, and of 6500 cases tried at Crown Court 4200 accused remained on bail.

Why? Two reasons. The first is that there is no room in the jails, and government cutback in public spending makes it unrealistic to expect sympathy for any demands for more jail accommodation for burglars. The second is the law itself. When prisons were under intolerable pressure, a new Bail Act was passed by Parliament in 1976, enforced in April 1978. The new law eased the situation; every arrested person is given a 'presumption in favour of bail', thus reversing a situation in which a defendant had to make out a case for the granting of bail. Under this new Act magistrates can only refuse bail if they are convinced the defendant may interfere with the course of justice, commit further crime or abscond.

All have been shown to be difficult areas which require increased skill in judgement by both magistrates and the judiciary in higher courts. It is easier to grant bail than to refuse. Therefore it is now vital that there should be much greater accountability by both magistrates and judges who have the power to grant or refuse bail.

This is where the Government should act to appoint an ombudsman. The ombudsman should keep records of all cases in which bail is granted, where bail is jumped and where further crime is committed while on bail. There can be no guarantee that people given bail will not commit further crime, but the system would identify those magistrates and judges who err more than others in their judgements. The fact that their performance would be under scrutiny would make them more accountable. Accountability is not only for those in the dock. It is also for those on the bench.

In my research I heard of a surprising number of incidents when large sums of money were lost and the police not told. A Scotland Yard detective said his guess, based on experience, was that an additional 10% could safely be added to official totals. That was the minimum, but he said he would not be surprised if this 'grey' area of crime was not substantially larger. I was told there were many reasons for not reporting burglaries. A small claim could result in insurers getting tougher. Other people write off minor break-ins rather than involve the police who have only a small chance of recovering the goods. To demonstrate his point, he introduced me to a long-standing contact, an east London publican.

Three weeks previously the publican had awakened in the morning to find his 'safe', a big steel cabinet, forced, and £6000 in cash stolen. A door had been forced to gain entry to the pub. The publican had not called the police. Instead, he had telephoned the Yard detective and requested an urgent 'private meeting'.

The publican's cash hoard had been the unofficial 'profits' from various till and drink-selling dodges, plus undeclared extra profits from the snack counter. None of the money had been declared for tax purposes, and the publican's fear of a close examination by tax and VAT men was much greater than the £6000 loss. His only consolation was that he was able 'privately' to tell the Yard man of his loss – and hope the local CID might keep a closer watch on his premises.

Only expert in-depth study by qualified researchers, spanning several years, could really expose the extent of unreported burglaries. In 1979 the first research of this type was launched by AGB Research Surveys of Great Britain. In a pilot probe interviewers visited a specimen 4000 homes. Three questions were put: (1) Have you been burglarised during the last twelve months? (2) Has there been an unsuccessful attempt to burglarise your home during this period? (3) If the answer to either of these questions is 'yes', did you report the incident to the police? For every 100 burglaries reported to the the police there were a further 37 successful burglaries not reported. In addition there were 58 unsuccessful attempts at burglary for every 100 reported successful burglaries. Just over half the unsuccessful attempts were reported to the police.

These results of a pilot sample indicated that the situation was far worse than believed. Sir Robert Mark suggested that the State's obligation to protect people effectively from burglary had been abandoned. Here was evidence indeed that this had already been taken to heart by a section of the public – understandable when considered against Scotland Yard's 'clear-up' rate in 1978: 10% over all, compared with 17% in 1973.

There is no doubt that Scotland Yard CID is directed by most astute and brilliant senior officers – men whom industry itself would consider invaluable. The new tactics making burglary a top priority in 1979/80 were a shrewd step, encouraged by provincial forces clearing up burglaries with 38% success. But there is no single action that can rectify the scandalous situation that has been allowed to

140

develop in burglary in particular and crime in general. Required action has to be manifold.

First, there must be far more police. This does not mean simply filling existing vacancies so that all forces are 'up to full strength'. A total re-examination of the authorised manpower of each force is required, for the 'authorised establishment' – which means the permitted strength – is totally unrealistic. The simple fact is that the number of police has fallen tragically behind the rate of crime. In 1971 there were 1,665,663 serious crimes in England and Wales. To cope with this there were 74,350 police (excluding the Metropolitan Police district which I will come to later). In 1978 there were 2,395,757 serious crimes, an increase of 730,094 offences. But there were only 85,650 police, or 11,300 more police, to deal with 730,094 more crimes. In the ten years from 1968, the authorised top manning level of police in England and Wales has only been increased from 82,093 to 91,079. Yet in the same period the number of serious crimes has rocketed from 1,407,774 to 2,395,757.

An even more dramatic example is provided by examining the Metropolitan Police manpower. In 1939 the force had 18,981 officers to deal with 94,852 crimes. These officers made 20,123 arrests for crime. By 1972 the volume of serious crime had virtually increased fourfold – to 354,445. Yet they have only 21,440 officers, a mere 2459 more than in 1939.

During the financial year 1978/9 Merseyside, which had the biggest drop in crime for a metropolitan area, also had easily the highest ratio of police officers per head of population (excluding London). Thus, evidence proves that a key factor in controlling crime is the number of police. As an example, in 1978 an enquiry into police pay had resulted in a major wage-increase. Across the nation men and women poured into recruiting-stations. Between January and July the police nationwide had a manpower growth of nearly 4000. The immediate result was that serious crime, including burglary, fell. In many areas there were really significant decreases. There was immediate rejoicing. But many top officers tempered their enthusiasm with caution. Previous experience has shown that rising crime can be stopped by positive action such as increased police manpower brought about by higher wages. Police history has shown that such events turn out to be only a pause, as though crime were resting before jumping to even more dizzy heights.

Another part of the police manpower problem is that the ratio of the police to the population as a whole has in this country been traditionally low. The reason has been the theory that law enforcement is a communal responsibility. In round terms, England and Wales have just over 100,000 police for 50 million citizens. Make allowances for shift duties, weekly and annual leave, illness and training, and this figure is reduced to a quarter. This means that at any one time there are only 25,000 officers physically on duty for a population of 50 million.

While the domestic population has had to sit back and suffer more and more crime, the industrial section has been able to help itself. Many thousands of firms found that the inadequacies of the police provided by government produced crime-losses that simply were not commerically acceptable. So they turned to private enterprise and bought their own private security at competitive prices. Across the nation an army emerged consisting of security guards aided by security dogs, patrol cars, armoured vehicles, and the best scientific gadgetry back-up that money could buy.

So what of the future for the police? Even with the much heralded but small manpower increases, the most the police can hope for in the 1980s is to continue to give inadequate service. It is not because the police themselves do not try their hardest. They are rightly described as the best in the world. The physical and moral courage needed to join a basically unarmed police service required to tackle increasing violence speaks for itself. But it is an inadequate service simply because there are too few for the problem.

Additionally, far too much is being asked of the police. Their performance, when considered against manpower and technical resources, is incredibly good; but the police service alone is totally inadequate for the problem, resulting in a considerable over-estimation of police ability to control crime. Mr Peter Engstad, a Canadian government criminologist, backed this conclusion during the 1979 conference of the Cambridge Institute of Criminology when he said: 'The argument that more police with better equipment responding even more rapidly to calls will effectively control crime has been discredited in the eyes of a growing number of police administrators and students of policing.'

His opinion is backed by the findings of Dr George Kelling of the Police Foundation in Washington. His research has shown that more men on patrol is not the total answer to the crime problem. Even the belief widely held by many British police chiefs that part of the answer is faster response to calls, producing more arrests and public satisfaction, must be seriously questioned. Research by Mr David Farmer of the United States Government's National Institute for Law Enforcement and Criminal Justice concludes that the number of arrests from fast police response is minimal. Many victims initially seek help and comfort from friends before calling police.

Police themselves, therefore, cannot provide the whole answer. The answer lies with the State and the community. As my research into burglars has shown, the State is very reluctant to imprison

142

burglars as an initial deterrent. The reason is that prisons are in a scandalously overcrowded condition. Only the really persistent burglar is given a custodial sentence. The limited prison accommodation mainly holds men of violence – the bank robber, the sex attacker, the men and women who 'mug' or beat up victims. If the State used prison as a deterrent and encouraged the judiciary to make a prison-sentence mandatory, prisons could not provide the accommodation. Again, the issue of more prisons, staff and ancillary social services is not a big vote-catcher for any government.

Furthermore, the figures for burglary show there are so many at the 'game' that, if more were arrested and jailed, this would create another major social problem. To make matters worse, employment prospects for those youngsters actually sent to Borstal or jail diminish substantially. The armed forces will not take them nor will many other official bodies. As criminologist Dr Donald West says in his book *The Young Offender* (1970), 'This kind of discrimination means that society as a whole has little faith in the reformative effect of penal treatment and little sense of obligation to try to make a place for anyone marked out as an official delinquent.'

So what can be done? The police are fully stretched: they solve less than half the burglaries. The jails are so full that it is not realistic to try to seek as a deterrent the loss of freedom. The solution must lie with both the community and commerce. Insurance companies who have so successfuly cashed in on the burglary business should devise more fiscal methods of encouraging 'customers' to help themselves. A far greater use of the inducement of 'no claims' bonuses would be an incentive. It has worked with motor transport. Why not have a system in which, for every year burglary is avoided by increased physical security and standard crime-prevention steps, such as remembering to check that all doors and windows are locked, there is a discount on the next premium? This would encourage people to be more crime-prevention conscious. They would be helping themselves with financial incentive, and there is need to enhance the involvement of the community in the control of crime.

There is a lot of purposeful activity already aimed at involving the community in protecting their homes and property. There are many local initiatives. In separate parts of the country, anti-burglary schemes of varying magnitude are run, with excellent results. But there is very little national co-ordination, so no effective over-all pattern has emerged. Now, more than ever before, there is need to adjust balance and distribution of crime-prevention resources.

Police forces, nationwide, urgently need to adopt a uniform policy. Chief constables do worry about their autonomy, but there is so much to be gained from working as one against a problem of such gigantic proportions. The adoption by some forces of a burglar-alarm policy based on the lessons learned by the West Midlands Constabulary is a step in the right direction, having saved the public large sums of money in some areas.

It is all patchwork. While police chiefs disagree over policy, while crime prevention lacks effective co-ordination, and while commerce avoids giving fiscal encouragement to those at risk, the burglar will contine to enjoy an unprecedented boom.

Appendices

I Burglary Law

Like all criminal law, burglary law has been devalued. The devaluation started with a blurring of the edges, steadily becoming even more blurred as, with the recent explosive rise in the prison population, judges are prevented from jailing the guilty. The courts' inability to impose custodial sentences, particularly for burglary, has actively encouraged crime; and offences which ten or fifteen years ago were regarded as very serious and were being tried at an Assize Court (now Crown Court) or Quarter Sessions are now being dealt with by magistrates. Offenders who only five years ago merited terms of imprisonment are now being given suspended sentences and probation orders. Burglary provides a dramatic example of this pattern.

There have been alarming changes in sentencing. Judges know that prisons are full, and are firmly reminded of it by the Court of Appeal. In consequence sentences of four years have been reduced to three years; sentences of three years are now two; two are nine months; and sentences of between nine and eighteen months are suspended.

This has not been in the public interest. It is simply because the jails are full and government has failed to provide secure accommodation to match the situation. What the law provides has become ineffective because of what government provides or, rather, what it fails to provide.

The public as a whole has not realised that this state of affairs exists. Only the victims of crimes discover it, too late. Victims of burglary, for example, find that their case is likely to be dealt with at any old court and the sentence most often certainly does *not* fit the crime.

Two political chiefs are directly responsible. The Lord Chancellor's Department is responsible for the appointment of judges and

145

the arrangements in the higher courts. There has been a succession of Lord Chancellors who have failed to stand up to and take on the masters of the purse strings at the Treasury. The result of the inadequate funding has been the appalling erosion of standards as far as trials are concerned: there has been too little building of new courts and funding for all the facilities needed. The result is long queues for justice – some cases waiting years for a hearing.

How can justice start to function when witnesses have to try to recall events that took place a year or so earlier? The Lord Chancellor's Department has been proven to lack political muscle and is no match for the Treasury.

The Home Secretary is responsible for magistrates, the police and prisons. Each succeeding Secretary has failed to get a proper share of central funds made available to counteract the devaluation of law and order. Strong ministers would have obtained the funds needed for more prisons and more attractive pay and conditions for those men and women needed to staff them. Increased police pay forced on a government by an independent review is only a short-term sop. The trouble is that law and order is a grey area, and the issues of more prisons, more courts, and many more policemen are said not to be the best of vote-catchers.

This need not be so. In 1978 the Conservative Prime Minister Mrs Margaret Thatcher gave important backing to law and order and demonstrated what a ready-made platform this is. But it has not been exploited adequately, despite the fact that British people are concerned about the law and maintenance of its standards.

What should be the concern of all people is the subtle change of standards, which is not necessarily happening with public approval.

The list below details the rich variety of options now open to courts when dealing with the guilty. Burglars and their legal advisors in making pleas for leniency know full well how to exploit the system to their advantage, and to the detriment of the standards of law and punishment.

Absolute or conditional discharge
An absolute discharge is used when the court, having found the offender guilty of the offence, considers no further action is required. For a conditional discharge, the offender remains liable to be sentenced for the original offence if he is convicted of a further offence within a period of not more than three years.

Probation order
An offender aged seventeen or over at the time of conviction may be put under the supervision of a probation officer for not less than six months and not more than three years. The order may include

146

additional requirements for attendance at a day training centre, residence for a specified period in a probation hostel or treatment for a mental condition.

Supervision order
A juvenile may be given a supervision order as a result of either criminal or care proceedings. The duration of the order may be up to three years and supervision is undertaken either by the local authority or a probation officer. Additional requirements may be made about the place of residence or treatment for a mental condition.

Fine
The maximum fine for adults which the Crown Court may impose is unlimited but the law prescribes for each offence the maximum fines that can be imposed by a magistrates' court. When imposing a fine (or later if the fine has not been paid) a magistrates' court may make a money payment supervision order placing the offender under the supervision of a person specified by the court.

Attendance centre order
Attendance centres are provided in most populous areas for boys under the age of seventeen and there are two senior attendance centres for young men aged seventeen and under twenty-one. The court specifies the total number of hours (between 12 and 24) for which a person is required to attend the centre.

Community service order
An offender aged seventeen or over may be given an order to carry out unpaid work in the community for between 40 and 240 hours during a period of twelve months.

Detention centre order
A male offender aged fourteen and under twenty-one may be detained in a detention centre for three or six months.

Borstal training
A sentence of borstal training is available for young offenders aged fifteen and under twenty-one. The court does not stipulate the period of training, which must be between six months and two years.

Suspended sentence of imprisonment
A court passing a sentence of imprisonment of not more than two years may suspend the sentence for a period of between one and two years. A court passing a suspended prison sentence of more than six

months may make a supervision order placing the offender under the supervision of a probation officer.

Imprisonment
The powers of the courts to pass sentences of imprisonment and the maximum available for each offence are specified by law. A magistrates' court may not impose a prison sentence of more than six months for one offence unless there is an express exclusion to the contrary. If consecutive terms of imprisonment are imposed for indictable offences tried summarily, there is an overall limit of twelve months.

Care order
A care order commits a child to the care of the local authority, giving the local authority the power and duties of a parent. The local authority has a duty to review the case every six months to consider whether to discharge the order.

Otherwise dealt with
Sentences include hospital orders, detention for juveniles under section 53 of the Children and Young Persons Act 1933 and 'no penalty'.

II Facts and Figures

The following official statistics (extracted from the *Statistics of the Criminal Justice System England and Wales 1968–78*) set out how in the last decade burglary has boomed, how the number of burglars caught by the police has declined, and the involvement of women in burglary.

There were 2½ million indictable offences of serious crime recorded in 1978. Of these 56 per cent were offences of theft and handling stolen goods and 22 per cent were offences of burglary. The breakdown of indictable offences by type is as follows:

Theft and handling stolen goods	56.0%
Burglary	22.0%
Criminal damage	12.0%
Fraud and forgery	4.8%
Violence against the person	3.4%
Sexual offences	0.9%
Robbery	0.5%
Other	0.1%

The increase in the number of indictable burglary offences recorded by the police in England and Wales (in thousands):

148

1969	1970	1971	1972	1973	1974	1975	1976	1977	1978
420.8	431.4	451.5	438.7	393.20	483.8	521.9	515.5	604.1	565.7

The clear-up rates by percentage, which show how few cases of burglary are solved:

1969	1970	1971	1972	1973	1974	1975	1976	1977	1978
34	36	37	37	37	34	34	34	31	32

Burglars try to avoid violence because they know that if arrested simply for burglary without violence they have an excellent chance of not being jailed. But below we see that in the last decade there has been a 100 per cent increase in the number of burglaries in which crooks are known to have carried firearms.

1969	1970	1971	1972	1973	1974	1975	1976	1977	1978
50	36	42	45	36	43	77	63	91	102

The large majority of burglars are released after arrest on bail. Only 22 per cent of people charged with burglary were kept in custody during and while awaiting trial. These figures show the persons remanded at magistrates' courts in 1978 and their remand status (in numbers of persons remanded and percentages):

Persons remanded as a percentage of persons proceeded against	Total number remanded (000s) = 100%	Proportion of total persons remanded		
		On bail throughout	Mixed remands	In custody throughout
52	40	69	9	22

Police experience is that many burglars, once released on bail, return to burglary. Some set out to collect nest-eggs from the proceeds of burglary in case they are jailed. Others carry on to pay for any future fine. A few thousand released on bail simply fail to turn up for their hearings. Persons released on bail by magistrates' courts who failed to appear to court bail in 1978:

Total number bailed by the court (000s)	Percentage failing to appear to court bail
31	3

Persons tried at the Crown Court (1978) for burglary and their remand status:

Persons remanded as a percentage of persons tried	Total number remanded (000s)=100%	Proportion of total persons remanded		
		On bail throughout	Mixed remands	In custody throughout
39	7	64	5	31

As burglars grow older they also become far more experienced – and much harder for the police to arrest. Police have their biggest success in arresting burglars aged between 14 and 17 years of age, followed by those aged 10 and under 14. The arrest rate for burglars aged 21 and over falls dramatically. The following table shows the proportion in percentages of offenders found guilty of, or cautioned for, burglary in 1978.

Males				Females			
Age 10–13	Age 14–16	Age 17–20	Age 21+	Age 10–13	Age 14–16	Age 17–20	Age 21+
23	25	18	11	6	6	5	2

More and more girls are taking an active part in crime of all types, but very few female burglars go to jail. Their biggest involvement is in handling stolen goods. Sentenced population, by sex and offence group (1978):

Males		Females	
Burglary	31%	Theft and handling stolen goods	36%
Theft and handling stolen goods	25%	Violence against the person	18%
Violence against the person	18%	Burglary	10%
Robbery	6%	Fraud and forgery	10%
Sexual offences	5%	Criminal damage	5%
Fraud and forgery	4%	Robbery	4%
Criminal damage	2%	Sexual offences	0.5%
Other	9%	Other	16.5%

No other group of criminals, apart from robbers, have as high a rate of previous convictions for similar offences. The percentages of males and females convicted in 1977 for violence against the person, sexual offences, burglary and robbery:

Principal offence of 1977 conviction	Total	Number of known previous convictions	
		0	1 or more
Males			
Violence against the person	100	40	60
Sexual offences	100	48	52
Burglary	100	29	71
Robbery	100	29	71
Females			
Violence against the person	100	71	29
Sexual offences			
Burglary	100	51	49
Robbery			

Index

false alarms, 112–14, 118–24
Farmer, Dr David, 142
Farrow, Linda, 59–60
fire-escapes, 19
flower-pots, 100–1, 104

garages, 100–1, 102–3, 106
Glasgow, 79, 126
Group 4 Total Security, 110
Guide to Home Contents Insurance, A,
    130–3
Guildford, 19, 88, 127

Hemel Hempstead, 127
Hickey, Michael, 61
Hickey, Vincent, 61
hi-fi, 16, 19, 21, 24, 46, 64, 65, 106, 129
high-risk areas, 97, 118, 125–7, 136–7
High Street: stolen goods in, 1, 68–9,
    70
Home Office, 79, 81, 113, 118, 125, 138

Ilford, 127
informers: burglars', 41–4, 77; police,
    60, 80
insurance, 3, 4, 12, 13–14, 16, 65,
    117–24, 125–37; up-valuing, 13–14,
    125–37; refusal to reinsure, 16;
    premiums, 16, 134, 135, 136–7;
    replacement-as-new, 16, 133;
    under-insurance, 127–8, 129–31;
    assessing, 131–3; indemnity, 133,
    136; index-linked, 133–4; no claims
    bonus, 134; advice on security, 137

jewellery, 8, 43, 46, 55
juveniles, 20–37, 92–3, 94, 96

Kelland, Assistant Commissioner
    Gilbert, 92, 93
Kelling, Dr George, 142
keys, 100–1, 104; keyholders, 122–3
Kilmarnock, 126
Kingston upon Thames, 127
Koenig, Della, 53

ladders, 8, 100–1, 102–3, 106
Lancaster, 126
Legal & General, 130, 134, 135
letter-boxes, 100–1, 102–3, 104
Liverpool, 126
Llandudno, 126
locks, *see* doors; windows
London, 1, 7–14, 15–17, 20, 22, 24, 25,
    29, 30, 33, 40–1, 44, 46, 48, 50, 51,

52–3, 54, 55, 57, 59, 61–2, 63–5, 66,
    71, 72, 73, 74, 88, 90–6, 111–12,
    126–7, 140

MacAlpine, Lady Philippa, 52, 54
McArthur, James 110
McNee, Commissioner Sir David, 90–6
Manchester, 17–18, 19, 68–9, 126
Mark, Sir Robert, 2–3, 16, 90, 140
Market Research Society, 44
Matthews, Chief Constable Peter, 58, 89
Modern Alarms, 109
money, 8, 17, 19, 21, 24, 43, 46, 50
Motherwell, 126
murder: burglary and, 59–61, 63

National Association of Local
    Government Officers, 136
National Farmers' Union, 136
National Supervisory Council for
    Intruder Alarms, 113–14
National Union of Teachers, 136

offices: burglary of, 18–19, 50, 137

paintings, 9, 41, 70–5
Paisley, 126
plate, 57
police, 117–24; stretched resources, 1,
    2–3, 10, 76, 96, 141, 143; arrest-rate,
    1, 3, 28, 89, 90–6, 140; anti-burglary
    squads, 3, 4, 76; Metropolitan, 9, 20,
    32, 61, 73, 74, 77, 78, 81, 87, 89,
    90–6, 112, 127, 141; Scenes of Crime
    Officers, 10, 74; 'Q' cars, 31–2, 83,
    85, 88; City of London, 74–5;
    collators, 79; Crime Prevention
    Officers, 106; West Midlands, 113,
    144; Dorset, 121; advice on security,
    137. *See also* informers; Scotland
    Yard
Police Foundation, Washington, 142
porcelain, 62, 106
Powis, Deputy Assistant Commissioner
    David, 92, 93, 95, 98; *Signs of Crime*,
    98–9
Preston, 114–15, 126
prisons, 1, 2, 50, 56, 69, 76;
    overcrowded, 139, 143

rape: burglary and, 13, 18, 42, 61–3
Reading, 127
receivers, 1, 29–30, 40, 66–75, 89
Redhill, 127
Rees, Detective Inspector Jeffrey, 52, 53

Robinson, James, 61
Romford, 41, 127

safes, 31–2, 33, 55
Scotland Yard, 2, 3, 10, 11, 14, 20, 21,
    28, 32, 42, 50, 52, 72, 74–5, 112,
    128, 130, 139, 140; Central Robbery
    Squad, 91; Criminal Intelligence
    Department (C11), 53, 78–86, 89;
    Criminal Investigation Department,
    32, 59, 73, 93–4, 95, 140; Flying
    Squad (C8), 30; Fraud Squad (C6),
    68; Murder Squad, 59–60; Policy
    Committee, 90; Serious Crimes
    Squad (C1), 78; Special Branch, 79;
    Special Patrol Group, 93; Specialist
    Robbery Squad, 90; Stolen Vehicle
    Squad (C10), 78; surveillance, 80–6;
    Traffic Department, 82. *See also*
    informers; police
Scott-Hall, James, 56
security, 1, 4, 106–14; door-chains,
    102–3, 104; door-viewers, 102–3,
    104; double-glazing, 106; guards, 4,
    110–12, 142; holidays, 15. *See also*
    alarms; doors; windows
self-protection, 114–16
Shrewsbury, 126
silver, 9, 32, 45, 65, 66–7
Slough, 127
Southworth, Jean, QC, 52, 54
statistics, 1, 2, 3, 4, 16, 61, 63, 75, 87,

88, 89, 90–112, 114, 117, 125, 126,
    137, 138–41
Surrey, 15, 19, 27, 58, 67, 87–9, 127
Sutton, 127

telephones: tapping, 66, 78, 79–80, 81;
    alarms linked to, 107, 110, 111, 116,
    120, 122, 123; silent dialling, 115
television sets, 9, 16, 17, 24, 26, 45, 65
Twickenham, 127

Underwood, Detective Chief
    Superintendent Ron, 87
United States of America, 47, 49;
    National Institute or Law
    Enforcement and Criminal Justice,
    142

vandalism, 9, 17–18, 18–19, 57
videotape-recorders, 9, 45

Warrington, 126
Watford, 127
West, Dr Donald: *Young Offender*, 143
Wigan, 127
windows: bars, 102–3, 104; locks,
    102–3, 104–6, 129, 134, 135, 137;
    louvre, 100–1, 102–3, 104;
    reinforced, 4, 16
Woods, Sir Colin, 91, 117

Yew Tree Farm, 61, 63